SOUTH CAMPUS - LIBRARY
TARRANT COUNTY JUNIOR COLLEGE
FORT WORTH, TEXAS 76119

A01550241001

ALAMO   AN IN-DEPTH STUDY OF T
HE BATTLE

HUNEYCUTT, C. D

F390.H948 1986

                              SC

BIND NOTED
2-23-94 KB

A01550241001

ALAMO   AN IN-DEPTH STUDY OF T
HE BATTLE

HUNEYCUTT, C. D

F390.H948 1986

SC

THE ALAMO

AN IN-DEPTH STUDY OF THE BATTLE

The Alamo chapel today. In the 1840s U.S. Army Engineers added the high center 'crown'. In 1836 the top was level.

BY

C.D. HUNEYCUTT

The Cover : *From a drawing done in 1836. Shows front of chapel, low wall in front of it, and part of 2 story barracks - as seen from southwest corner of outer wall.*

This book is dedicated to:

U.S. Army Major Arthur Nicholson, an Observor, who was shot in East Berlin on March 24, 1985, and allowed to bleed to death by refusing him any medical aid.
The next time you see smiling Russians on T V ... remember Major Nicholson.

Copyright 1986 by C.D. Huneycutt
All Rights Reserved
ISBN 0 915153 12 2

FORWORD

It is impossible to understand the Alamo battle without connecting it in time and enfluence to the Napoleonic Wars. 1836 was very much in Napoleon's shadow. It was an extensive shadow. Nearly everything which happened in the Alamo battle is covered by it.

It was Napoleon who sold Louisiana to Jefferson, thus making the western migration possible. Napoleon encouraged the breakup of Spain's colonies in the Americas. especially Mexico. Little wonder that Santa Anna modeled his army and strategy after him.

And look at the Americans in the Alamo. They were there because of the 20-24 cannon ! Cannon were the key to Napoleon's military tactics. It had been his branch of service and it was French mastery of artillery, more than any other factor, which brought those first years of victory across Europe.

Cannon could win battles and cannon within forts could block armies. It was this knowledge which impressed men like Travis, Bowie, Jameson, and Dickinson. They were awed by those tubes of brass and iron. So awed they thought they could use them to block a Dictator's army and save the Texans in the interior.

Had not Sidney Smith stopped Napoleon's Egyptain campaign at Acre with mud walls and cannon ? Had not countless sieges in Spain against crumbling missions and old castles decided the fates of campaigns ?

As we shall see, Napoleon's ghost was at the Alamo. So were his tactics. Without this new perspective there can be no real understanding of what happened at the Alamo.

AUTHOR'S NOTE:

I accumulated so much additional material related to the Alamo battle that I had to decide either to divide it into essays or to let it gather dust. In the interest of Alamo enthusiasts I have decided the former. And it will be titled THE ALAMO BATTLE: 8 ESSAYS.

December, 1986

C.D. Huneycutt

I would like to thank Faith Efird of the Albemarle library for her assistance in securing inter-library loans of books & documents. Texas libraries were especially helpful: Mr. Gracy of the Texas State Library at Austin. Excellent staff work there located their LIBRARY CHRONICLE with the article by Helen Hunnicut. Thanks to Beverly McFarland of the Eugene C. Barber Texas History Center; Cynthia J. Beeman, Research Assistant at the Texas State Archives, Texas State Library at Austin, Texas.

BACKGROUND : SANTA ANNA

Born on February 21, 1794, into what we would call a middle class family. He was sent to a military school when 14. Spanish military ideas were soon supplimented by new ones from Spain's 7 year struggle with Napoleon.

When 17, Santa Anna was transferred to the cavalry. That branch was usually filled with upper class sons. How he or his parents were able to effect the transfer isn't known. But it was a huge step on his way to becoming an officer. On October 7, 1812, one year after the transfer, he became a 2nd Lieut.

In June 1813, an event occurred which probably molded his attitude toward Anglo-Americans as fighters. He was serving under Spanish general Arredondo when the province of Coahuila declared their independence. Arredondo had 735 infantry and over 1200 cavalry. Not far from San Antonio, near the Medina River, they ambushed 850 American and Mexican rebels.

Arrendondo followed the usual Napoleonic tactics; he sent out skirmishers who engaged the rebels and retreated to draw them into a trap. Arredondo closed this trap with a band playing the *'Deguello'* which meant 'no mercy' and, for the Spanish, was appropriate because in their eyes these enemies had no military status (i.e. flag, recognized country, etc) and were therefore to be made examples of to discourage future rebellions.

The trapped Americans among the rebels fought hard but then tried to retreat. Exactly what the cavalry was waiting for. Napoleonic tactics called for cavalry to annihilate a retreating foe. Fleeing men on foot were no match for sabre swinging horsemen and lances.

The cavalry captured 80 rebels. Trees were laid across a ditch and the captured forced to balance on the trees as firing squads shot at them. Here 19 year old Santa Anna was given proof that Napoleonic tactics worked. Skirmishers, cannon (2 were used in the ambush), bands playing, running Americans, and no quarter for prisoners. Result: A quick, decisive, and complete victory. I must point out, however, that Napoleon publicly decried any execution of prisoners. But during his Egyptian campaign he did order thousands of Turkish prisoners to be killed.

Arredondo went on to San Antonio. This would be Santa Anna's first visit to this small Mexican town. 300 people were jammed in a small jail. Many were executed the next morning. The town was looted and the women abused by the troops.

Santa Anna then spent several years hunting anti-government guerrilla bands in Mexico. He commanded the force which defeated Francisco de Paula - for which he became Captain. More Mexican rebels were hunted down. He then joined the revolution against the Spanish Viceroy because the man was too liberal. Santa Anna and the other officers wanted to preserve their own privilages.

In one of the last battles against the Viceroy's forces Santa Anna had his Bugler blow the *Deguello* while his men stormed Cordoba.

Also in 1822, Santa Anna proclaimed Mexico a Republic. He was financed by wealthy Spanish merchants. Especially those of Vera Cruz. Most officers belonged to the Scottish Rite Masons. Santa Anna's brother ran one of their newspapers and Santa Anna also joined.

In 1824, he married the daughter of a rich Vera Cruz Spanish merchant. He was moving in the right direction. He had learned where the money and power were in Mexico.

An old veteran of Napoleon's campaigns, a Frenchman named Jean Garnot, had been filling Santa Anna's head with visions of grandeur. A chance to live those visions occurred in 1829, when Spain invaded Mexico with 4,000 men near Tampico. The news was music to his ears. Without waiting for orders he put 2,000 soldiers onto ships at Vera Cruz and sailed for Tampico. Jean Garnot said, "This expedition may do for you what Napoleon's Egyptian campaign did for him." How right he was!

At 10 P.M., August 20, Santa Anna attacked the Spanish garrison at Tampico in 3 columns. It would have been a surprise attack except one man accidently fired a gun. The aroused Spanish garrison fought from windows and roofs. The sick and wounded were placed in positions from which they could fire.

By the next afternoon the typhoid riddled garrison was down to 1200 fighting men. But the Mexican flag was only above a few houses within the port city. That night Santa Anna attacked a fort in the harbor only to fail.

The Spanish commander asked for and was given a surrender with weapons and safe passage to Cuba. Notice that in dealing with a recognized enemy force he kept his word and acted honorably. His constant bombardment of Spanish positions had also been a factor. His adjustant in this first major victory was a Spanish veteran of the Peninsular War, General Castrillon. Remember that name well. We shall meet him again at the Alamo.

Now followed years of revolts against Mexican presidents. Like frogs they jumped one after the other to and from the President's desk in Mexico City. As the leading military commander (and now a hero) , Santa Anna was soon in a position to control which frog sat behind that desk and for how long. The General now would have time to play the role he wanted : Napoleon.

In early 1834, he changed his mind once and for all concerning what kind of government Mexico needed. Perhaps in this he was a realist:

"... I threw up my cap for liberty with great ardor, and perfect sincerity, but very soon found the folly of it. A hundred years to come my people will not be fit for liberty. They do not know what it is, unenlightened as they are, and under the influence of a Catholic clergy, a despotism is the proper government for them, but there is no reason why it should not be a wise and virtuous one."

Exactly what Napoleon became in France ! Both men would claim to be enlightened despots. Both men backed by the Catholic church.

It was in 1833, that Santa Anna began his collection of Napoleonic pictures, statues , and books. They filled his mind with ideas and gave him a role model. In April, 1834, he gained the support of the Catholic church. They agreed to give him money and he agreed to restore their power to collect for Masses, funerals, weddings, baptisms, etc.

On March 31, 1835, Santa Anna passed a law disbanding local militias. It was to disarm any local resistance to his dictatorship. This was the last straw for the northern provinces of Zacatecas and Texas. They needed local military forces to fight Indians. To disband would also place them at the mercy of the distant regular army of Mexico.

Both Texas and Zacatecas had hoped to retain their continued representation guarenteed by the Mexican Constitution of 1824. But Santa Anna wanted a centralized government in which he would have all the power.

Zacatecas revolted and he led an army of 3,500 to the capitol city Zacatecas to face a Mexican rebel army of 5,000. It was a easy victory with the city turned over to his troops as their reward. Special hatred was shown to Anglo-Americans. Women were again abused. Meanwhile the Catholic church was giving him 40,000 pesos a month.

In Texas, things were heating up. Stephen Austin had been in Mexico trying to win back some of the rights lost when Santa Anna had scrapped the 1824 Constitution. As late as January 1835, he had believed Santa Anna was a liberal ! By freeing Austin from a Mexican jail the Dictator probably hoped to decieve him as to his real intentions toward Texas. It backfired. When Austin returned to Texas he was *violently* anti-Santa Anna.

After his defeat of the Zacatecas rebels the Dictator must have watched the growing Texas rebellion with great humor. 23 years ago he had seen them easily defeated. Best of all, they were wealthy. General Almonte had toured Texas and written a glowing report of the extensive ranches, livestock, and small industries owned by the Anglo-Americans. So where he had used 3,500 troops to crush Zacatecas he sent 1500 under his brother-in-law General Cos to San Antonio to put down the rebellion.

Santa Anna in 1835 was a competent military man who had almost never (twice) lost a battle and *never* lost a campaign. He was now a dictator with the resources of 8 million people behind him. And the money of the Catholic church. At last he could indulge his dream of playing Napoleon.

The curtains on the stage of history were slowly opening. The first major actors were playing their parts. Soon the vast steppes of Texas would beckon this new Napoleon just as the steppes of Russia had beckoned the former 23 years earlier.

Antonio Lopez de Santa Anna would be president of Mexico 11 times.

David Crockett had this 'likeness' done in 1835.

Jim Bowie. Unquestionably the best leader in the Alamo but his illness forced him to back 26 yr. old Travis.

BACKGROUND : THE TEXANS

There were some 30,000 Anglo-Americans in the Spanish province of Texas by 1835. [1] They had been allowed in by past Spanish governments to tame the Indians and to establish settlements which could then be taxed. There were only some 3,000 hispanics in Texas. A number of abandoned missions reminded them that the central government was far away.

Santa Anna's staff officer, Almonte, had visited Texas in 1834. Santa Anna had sent him to report on the immigrants. I notice the report keeps mentioning how much their property is *worth* ! [2] It must have dawned on the Dictator that any campaign against them could be made profitable simply by seizing that wealth.

The Texans have been described as *clannish*.[3] This is probably a feature of any frontier people anywhere. As a military consideration it should be pointed out that the best fighting units number about 10.[4] In any company of 100 men there will be about 10 groups which socialize mainly with each other.(i.e. peer groups). Studies have shown that men in these small groups will fight extremely hard as long as they are together and in visual contact with each other.[5] They are fighting for their *GROUP* [6] - for those they consider their peers. Therefore, the Texans, by being 'clannish', possessed an important military attribute.

The Texas militia units were all armed with flintlock rifles in 1835. One military writer says any flintlock in America after 1835 was considered obsolete because guns were being converted to percussion.[7] But we have an eyewitness among those Texas militias and he says 'flintlock rifles.'[8] Plus, flint is easier to obtain than percussion caps in a frontier setting.

Soon to be entering Texas would be some volunteer units with a different weapon.(i.e. New Orleans Grays) They were financed and equipped by the citizens of New Orleans. Uniforms were gray with flat topped, woolen caps featuring glazed leather visors. They were not armed with rifles. A rifle was a hunting tool. Few American soldiers *ever* carried a rifle during this period. Scouts and militias which were attached to the army did carry them but not the soldiers wearing American uniforms.

So what were these volunteer companies armed with ? The accepted military weapon of the day: flintlock muskets and bayonets. Probably the U.S. Model 1816. These were 69 Caliber and except for some unique features were similar to the Brown Bess muskets of the Mexicans.

Cherokee chief Bowls saw some of these uniformed men in Nacogdoches and asked, "Are those Jackson's men ?"[9] The point I am making is that our idea of buckskined men with long rifles defending the Alamo is mostly wrong. A large number wore gray uniforms and all would use the large number of muskets left by General Cos after his surrender.

The advantage of the musket is that it can fire three times a minute while the rifle can only be loaded and fired once. Paper cartridges slide easily down those wide musket bores while small, patched, rifle balls must be rammed down those long, deep grooved rifle barrels. And rifles have to be cleaned after 10 shots because the grooves fill with powder residue. I have seen muskets fired over 50 times without cleaning.

That the U.S. Model 1816 was probably the basic Texan musket used in the revolution is confirmed by their order in 1840 of 1,500 from a arms contractor in Philadelphia.[10] The tight budget would have demanded they obtain only a weapon they had confidence in.

When we look at the Texan military structure in late 1835 we have to shake our heads. Here were desperate men - perhaps 2,000 at the most - from a population of 30,000 (remember families had 8-10 children) who were soon going to face regular armies from a country of 8 million. The Texans had no cavalry, no artillery, no *trained* regular army. All they had were groups of local militias. To fight the superb Mexican cavalry their mounted riflemen had to dismount ! As for guerrilla warfare on open steppes - difficult.

Their only chance was :

A. Get quick military help from trained volunteer units from outside Texas.
B. Fight from fortified positions where small numbers could withstand large forces.
C. Form their own Regular Army.
D. Gain time to create 'C'.

After the Dictator's defeat, when the rest of his ruined army was in retreat, Lt. Colonel Pena was talking one night near Goliad with two Americans. He told them,"There will be a future campaign in which a nation (Mexico) would be victorious against a handful of men..."[11] What he was saying was that in this past campaign they *had* been beaten by 'a handful.'

Napoleon's generals could add a warning :

"An invasion against an exasperated people, ready for all sacrifices and likely to be aided by a powerful neighbor, is a

dangerous enterprise, as well proved
by the war in Spain."[12]

One of my History professors decried the
Texan rebellion against Mexico, saying that
Texas *belonged* to Mexico - not to the Anglo-
Americans. Well, I would like to know WHICH
Indian tribe sold Texas to Spain and WHEN
this historic transaction occurred ? Then I
want to know when Mexico bought the same land
from Spain ?

If Mexico had the right to rebel against
Spain and claim the Spanish lands - then the
Texans also had the same right to rebel
against Mexico and claim the same land.

Just as the American colonists in 1776
had the right to rebel against the King of
England so the Texans in 1835 had the right
to rebel against a dictator who was depriving
them of their rights under the Mexican Constitution of 1824.

The Mexican people were betrayed in 1835
by their leaders. Just as they have been betrayed ever since. They were duped into
fighting against the Texans when they should
have been fighting *for* them and *for* the Constitution of 1824.

NOTES

1. P.119, Billington, THE FAR WESTERN FRON-
     TIER.
2. Pp.50-60, Morphis, HISTORY OF TEXAS.
3. P.118, DeShields, TALL MEN WITH LONG RIFLES.
4. P.293, Holmes, ACTS OF WAR : BEHAVIOR OF...
5. Ibid.
6. P.299, Ibid.
7. P.175, Held, THE AGE OF FIREARMS.

8. P.10, DeShields, TALL MEN...
9. P.121, Morphis, HISTORY OF TEXAS.
10. P.133, Gluckman, IDENTIFYING OLD MUSKETS...
11. P.184, Pena, WITH SANTA ANNA IN TEXAS.
12. P.23, Jomimi, ART OF WAR.

U.S. MODEL 1816 Musket featured brass flashpan. 69 Caliber. The "1822" musket was still the 1816 model according to Gluckman.

N.C. BORDER RIFLE was small bore and very accurate. Type probably carried by Crockett.

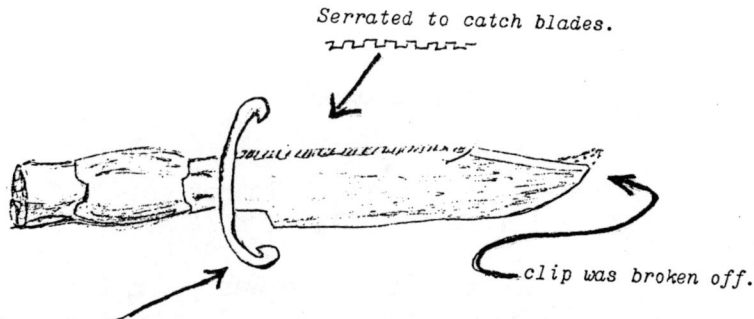

Serrated to catch blades.

clip was broken off.

Notched guards to hold blades.

The Moore Knife *with many unusual features might be one of Bowie's knives. Total length 13 inches.*

15

BACKGROUND:
THE ALAMO PERSONALITIES

WILLIAM BARRET TRAVIS

Born in Alabama. Left his wife necause he thought she was unfaithful and went to Texas to practice law. He became antagonistic with local Mexican authorities. They arrested him without 'due process' and he was finally released when friends traded a Mexican officer for him.

Travis belonged to the 'War Party' - as opposed to those still advocating peace. His diary of 1833-1834 has not *one* word about his politics. Either it was written during a lull in his activities or he was careful not to write anything which might be used to incriminate him.

The fact is that Major Bradburn was so terrified of Travis after he was released that this officer *hid* in the nearby woods because Travis had once sworn while Bradburn's prisoner to get even.[1] Travis was a leader because he knew how to talk. He was dangerous because he was so stubborn.

A entry in his diary:

"...Prairie so boggy - could not go - *THE FIRST TIME I EVER TURNED BACK IN MY LIFE.*"[2]

This was the man Fate was going to place in command of the Alamo. If a contest had been held in all Texas in 1835 to choose the most stubborn men - Willian B. Travis would have been among the winners. He numbered the women he had 'affairs' with and stopped numbering after meeting Rebecca Cummings.

On Jan. 11, 1834, he read "*COURT AND CAMP OF BONAPARTE.*" More importantly, (I think) he read "*SCOTTISH CHIEFS*" February 19-20, of the same year. Some puzzling events at the Alamo can be solved by referring to this book. His diary shows he liked good clothes and white hats. He was also able to write and speak Spanish, especially the former since he translated land titles and court documents.

Travis arrived at the Alamo on February 3, 1836, with 30 men. Bowie was already there with Captain Neill and over 80 men.[3] Mainly of the New Orleans Grays' First Company. Neill left to see after his family, turning command over to Travis. The men were furious. They voted and made Bowie their commander. Most of these men had never seen Travis before. But Travis and Bowie knew each other because his diary shows Bowie had been a client.[4] We don't know what they thought of each other. Bowie was a very wealthy man while Travis was a stubborn lawyer in love with a frontier girl.

Travis looked at the cannon in the Alamo. He had to have been impressed. This was the largest collection of artillery between the Mississippi and Rio Grande. Cannon fascinated civilians. Battles with cannon were in history books and one could become famous with them. To a romantic like Travis their appeal must have been enormous.

So Travis decided it was militarily important to hold this position against the next Mexican army which was expected to come by mid March. Travis had thus made a decision and this was a man who did not and would not change his mind. But he was wrong about one small thing. The Mexican army was coming fast and the Dictator driving it wanted vengeance for the defeat Cos had just suffered in San Antonio.

JAMES (JIM) BOWIE:

Born in South Carolina. The family moved to Lousiana. The Bowie boys were given a good education by their mother. Jim Bowie was a walking contradiction. He knew how to make money by taking chances - whether by selling slaves or buying and reselling land - money seemed to leap into his hands. But there was another side to him. He loved action. Perhaps it was an extension of his gambling instinct.

A neighbor of the Bowies later said he remembered Jim because he had, "a physical dexterity unlike any other man."[5] Bowie was a frontier gladiator. He loved knives.

In a conversation with Jeff Morey, who has seen the Moore knife, he pointed out that Bowie says in a letter, "...I lost one of my knives." And it makes sense that a man who liked and used knives would have several. This brings us to the Moore knife. In 1890 it was used by a Mexican to pay a debt. Said he had been one of Santa Anna's soldiers and on lifting Bowie's body to place it on the cremation wood - it fell out and he saved it. The knife was then used as a digging tool for some fifty years, breaking off the point.[6] No one seems to agree on whether this is *THE* knife Bowie had at the Alamo. One criticism made was that Bowie, being wealthy, wouldn't have had such a 'cheap' knife. But Jeff says there are traces of silver plating on the unique guards. It certainly is a fighting knife unlike any other pattern I have seen. And the guards and serrated top of the blade definately make it a knife to be used against other knives. If it isn't *the* Alamo knife, it certainly could be *one* of Bowie's knives.

Bowie had manners. Alan Ladd in "IRON MISTRESS" was close. He charmed the powerful

Veramendi family in San Antonio and walked away with the man's blond daughter, Ursula. Mexicans respect manners and good blood. Bowie was like a iron hand in a velvet glove.

Once in a church meeting some big mouths began turning the young minister's sermon into a comedy sketch. Bowie stood and announced in a solf voice what he would do if they didn't shut up. Then he added, "...I'm Jim Bowie."[7] The silence during the rest of the sermon was such that people were afraid to cough.

Bowie was a leader because he just always seemed to know what to do. With 20 men he once ambushed 300 Mexicans and soon had their surrender.[8] In the Conception Fight he deployed his outnumbered men, driving off the large attacking force and capturing their cannon. In the Grass Fight he was among the first in the saddle to intercept the Mexicans. I mention the above to show that Jim Bowie was not a frontier lout with a big knife. He was polished, he was rich, and he was a man everyone wanted to follow.

But his blond wife and their two children had died a few years ago in a cholera epidemic. Died because Bowie sent them where he thought they would be safe. Instead, he sent them to their deaths. Bowie drank now. Guilt haunted him and he found no peace. He and the others had taken San Antonio from General Cos and his name was on the Dictator's list. Time was running out.

DAVID CROCKETT :

Born in the western borderlands of North Carolina in 1786. (Sorry - it wouldn't be Tennessee for another 10 years) He grew up in a area embroiled in the Whisky Rebellion. He grew up among a people who hated authority: the Scotch Irish. His father ran a tavern and it was there Crockett learned about people and he learned to remember and tell stories.

By 1810, he had acquired a favorite rifle which he would call 'Betsy' - probably after his older sister. On the western N.C. border there were a number of gunsmiths making guns that were cheap but efficient. Crockett was poor and would remain so all his life. He would have acquired a simple, iron mounted, patchboxless, flintlock of about 32-38 caliber. Notice that when the Whigs gave him a fancy, silver mounted rifle, he called it 'pretty Betsy.' This in itself tells us his older flintlock was a plain border gun. I have seen these guns : set triggers and fine sights.

Notice that in his 1835 Biography he must shoot each bear twice. This tells me he used a small bore which was typical of these guns. Many were made without buttplates to reduce weight and a simple hole in the stock was the grease or wax receptacle for the patches.

Crockett was a simple man who liked to entertain people with frontier humor. Going to Congress was not his idea but that of a wealthy supporter who liked him. He stood for the squatters - the poor who had no legal claim to the lands they developed because they had no money to buy the land. He felt it was theirs by right of possession. Therefore, he supported Indian claims to their tribal lands because they were in the same position as the squatters who voted for him.

The Whig Party opposed Jackson's Democrats. In Crockett they saw a possible rival for Jackson's frontier brand of popularity. But there was a big difference. Jackson was now rich and the Democrats were powerful. Crockett had begun his political career as a friend of Jackson but not for long. And Andrew Jackson never forgave anyone who joined his enemies.

In 1834, Crockett wrote:

"... (Jackson) is surrounded by a lot of drunks & vermin that would destroy the country to provide their own interests..."

And in the same letter:

"But we have one hope the Senate will save the Constitution and laws in spite of King Andrew the First."[9]

In 1835, he would exclaim:

"Look at my neck, you will not find there any collar, with the engraving

> MY DOG.
>
> ANDREW JACKSON.

[10]

Forgive me if I dwell too long on Crockett. I have for many years been struggling with a historical novel on the man. As to his military experience Crockett had served in a mounted rifleman unit (scouts) attached to Jackson's regular army during the Creek Indian War in 1811. Something happened when they stormed a big Indian fort which would stay with Crockett ever after. Once the walls were taken the Indians retreated into a house and what could have been a bloody fight for this building was ended by setting fire to it - with 46 Indians inside ![11] The incident is probably behind his Alamo statement (repeated many times, according to Mrs. Dickinson):

"We should march out and die in the
open. I don't like to be penned up." [12]

Penned up like those Creek Indians who had defended a fort which was stormed - just as now this fort (Alamo) was about to be stormed.

Crockett was also active in that frontier club called the militia. It was a social thing and even small boys practiced marching and drilling with sticks as they watched their fathers and older brothers. In one of these units Crockett became 'Colonel.'

While the regular army drill was changed in 1812, I an sure the older 1895 regulation drill was still practiced in the frontier areas. With former military men as officers these units would have used the older drill.

What I am getting at is that when 'Col.' Crockett and 12 men arrived at the Alamo[13] on February 11, 1836, each of those riflemen *also* knew regular army drill due to prior militia training. In addition to their own rifles they could use the extra muskets and bayonets surrendered by Cos.

When Crockett arrived in San Antonio he was with relatives and friends - and people picked up along the way. He would even write his son, saying:

"...do not be uneasy about me I am with my friends..."[14]

Crockett was 49. He had come to Texas to get away from politics. To make a fresh start for himself. He and his men had earlier signed up as part of the 'regular' army of Texas. In his last letter he says he hopes to be elected to a future Constitutional convenion in Texas.[15] Perhaps there was some political life left in the Old Fox, after all.

A 12 year old boy in Little Rock said that when Crockett passed through he wore a *foxskin* cap. Would a 12 year old know the difference between a fox and a coonskin ? I think so. Crockett had thrown away the coonskin cap he had worn as a Congressman. Now he was the ole' Fox.

In Von Schmidt's painting of the Alamo battle Crockett is given a garrison cap like the Grays wore. Someone should get that ridiculous thing off Crockett's head. Many others in the Alamo wore those caps. But a Mexican Captain remembered:

"(one man) wore a buckskin suit and a cap all of a pattern entirely different from those worn by his comrades...This man I later learned was known as 'Kwockey.'" [16]

While in Little Rock, he attended an shooting match. They shot at 'X's back then, aiming for the center. He put 2 bullets in the center - one on top of the other ! There was nothing wrong with the ole' Fox's eyes.

In Crockett's group I suspect there was a paid informer. A agent keeping the Democrats informed of Crockett's movements and actions. He was much too important to let out of sight in - of all places - Texas ! Crockett himself would say they had been betrayed.[17] For someone who knew Jackson's 'Imps' (that's what he called them) nothing was impossible.

Crockett... A wild card that drifted by merest whim of fate onto the stage at the Alamo. A card Jackson's forces later tried to deface. But a card that will never be forgotten. The ole' Fox would become - through his humorous little booklets (' Almanacs') - a legend. He was among the last of his kind - the Scotch Irish frontiersmen whose way of life was fading fast in the 1830's.

So on our stage we have <u>Travis, the Romantic revolutionary. Bowie, the dying gladiator. Crockett, representing the last of the Trans-Appalachian Indian fighters</u>. They seem like characters out of a Garde B movie. But by mid-February they were all at a place in the middle of nowhere called Bexar. One observation about this place soon to be called San Antonio: As travelers approached, the white, sun bleached walls of the town and old mission seemed to glow. One traveler thought it a city of white marble.[18] Today the Alamo chapel is a gray, dirty looking monument. In 1836 it was part of a brightly white mission. In one sense these frontier pilgrims were coming to the 'Jerusalem' of Texas.

NOTES

1. Texas ALMANAC, 1859, as told by N.D. Labadie.
2. Entry for March 9, 1834.
3. P.71, Myers, John, THE ALAMO.
4. Entry for Dec. 28, 1833.
5. P.62, Myers, John, THE ALAMO.
6. P.28, Winter, Butch, "The Real Bowie...", THE NATIONAL KNIFE MAG., Aug. 1983. Also see "Is This The Knife..." by Jim Williamson, THE NATIONAL KNIFE MAG., Dec. 1983.
7. P.61, Myers, John, THE ALAMO.
8. Pp.65-66, Ibid.
9. Letter of Crockett, dated May 26, 1834.
10. P.211, Narrative of the Life of David Crockett by Crockett.
11. Pp.88-89, Ibid.
12. P.175, Morphis, HISTORY OF TEXAS.
13. P.98, Myers, John, THE ALAMO.
14. P.87, Tinkle, Lon, THE ALAMO.
15. Ibid.

16. P.163-164, DeShields, TALL MEN...
17. P.177-178, Hough, Emerson, THE WAY TO THE WEST.
18. P.61, Sibley, Marilyn, TRAVELERS IN TEXAS.

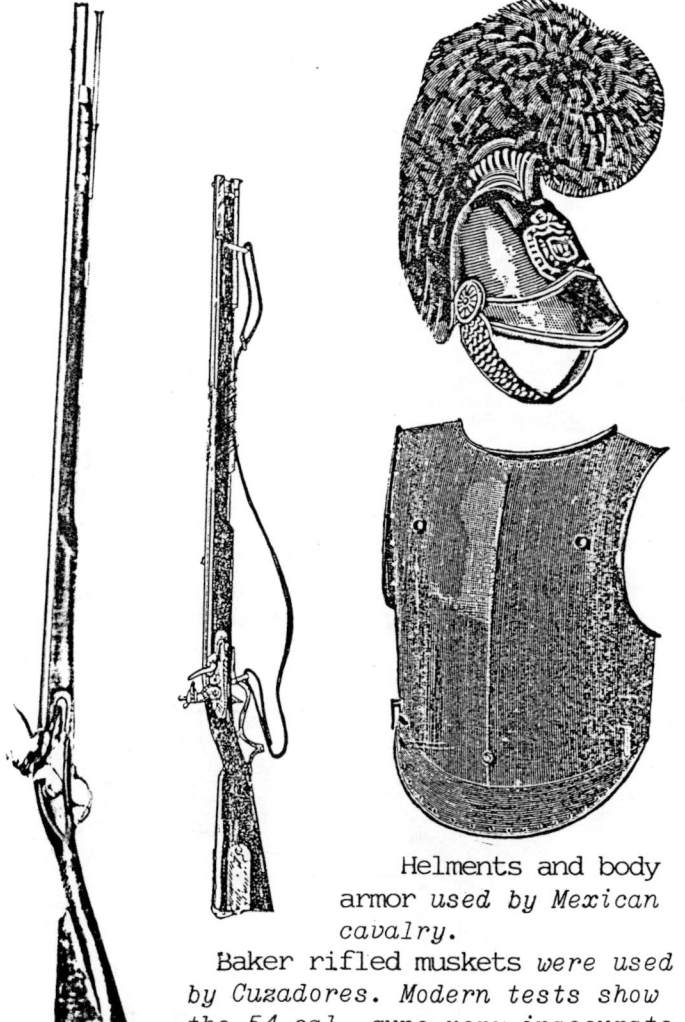

Helments and body armor *used by Mexican cavalry.*

Baker rifled muskets *were used by Cuzadores. Modern tests show the 54 cal. guns very inaccurate.*

British Brown Bess Muskets *were standard Mexican firearms for Texas campaign. 69 Cal. and very dependable. Carried 18 in. Bayonet.*

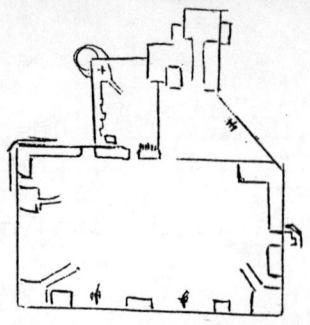

Map A. *Drawn on March 3, by a Mexican Engineer. Shows ditches outside northeast wall. (Map from Barker Texas Hist. Center, Univ. of Texas/Austin.)*

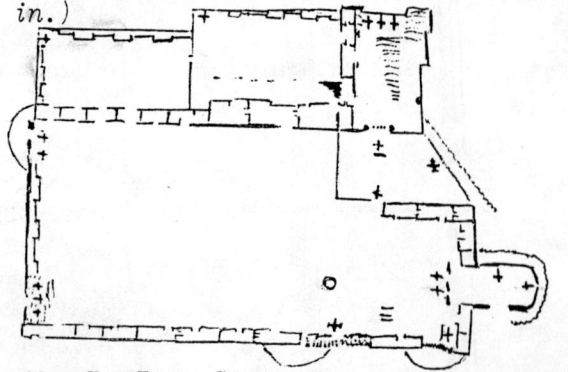

Map B. *From Capt. Navarro's 2nd Ed. 'The Texas War.' Shows the Alamo as he remembered it on March 6.*

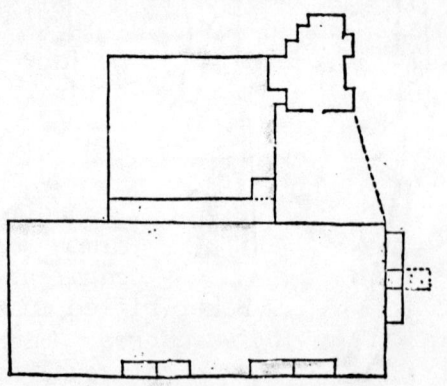

Map C. *R.M. Potter's map from "actual measurements." But outer dimensions have to be incorrect.*

BACKGROUND: THE ALAMO

General Cos had done the future defenders a great service. His 1500 men had worked hard on the mission before surrendering after his position in the town was overrun by Texan rebels in December. Cos never used his Alamo defenses.

Captain Navarro was sent by Cos to sign the surrender. This humiliation made Navarro furious. His detailed drawing of the old mission as he remembered it on March 6, will tell us how the defenders made some adjustments to their fort.

Cos turned the old mission into a fortress. Without the many weeks of hard labor by his men the Americans could never have held the Alamo as long as they did. Perhaps this fact rankled Capt. Navarro. He had seen those improvements made and then seen his commander surrender the modified Alamo without a test.

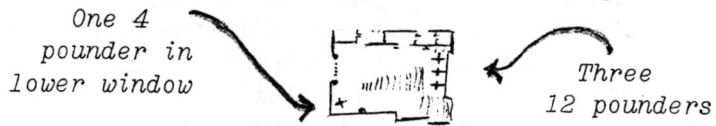

One 4 pounder in lower window

Three 12 pounders

POSITION #1
The chapel defenses

A inclined ramp was made and three cannon were wheeled to the top, pointing east. Notice here that the Mexicans are concentrating their guns into groups to enable fewer experienced men to operate them. Military manuals' of the period required 6-8 men per piece but in grouping them, each piece could be reloaded as it recoiled. A feature no doubt used later by Texans.

Unfortunately the roof had collapsed and mortars could make this position impossible to defend. The chapel could not be used as a 'last stand' defense. Those 4 foot walls were the thickest in the mission but absence of an roof made it a death trap.

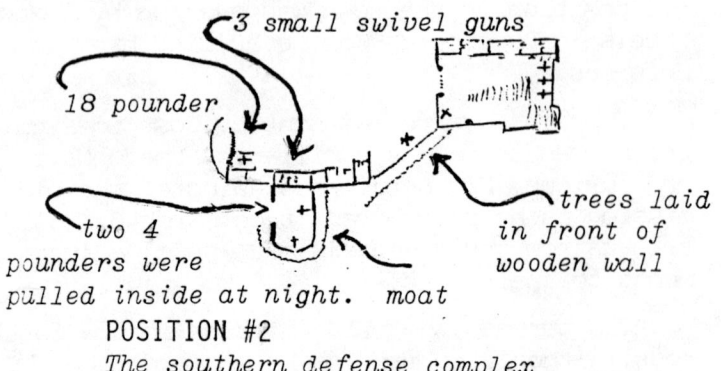

POSITION #2
The southern defense complex

Here the Mexicans had built a wooden wall to link the chapel to the adobe wall of the low barracks. When the mission was built it was decided to enclose the south gate (at that time the only gate) with buildings on each side. Holes were bored in the walls facing the gate to enable 'Christian' Indians to defend this gate against 'Wild' Indians. Cos had built a barricade outside this entrance to aid defense.

Above this gate the building called the Low Barracks rose in a "watch tower" above the entrance. In that high 'tower' were loop holes for 3 small caliber swivel guns. Friar Morfi mentions this feature which he saw in 1778.[1] This very same position with the same swivel guns will be mentioned later by a Mexican officer during the battle.[2]

Remember that most cannon in the Alamo were probably iron Spanish pieces. The exceptions might have been some small bronze cannon Cos had brought along.

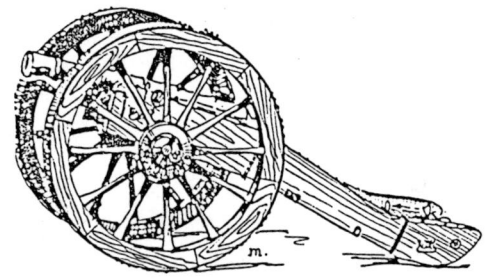

Spanish Field Artillery
*(Drawing by Albert Manucy from
ARTILLERY THROUGH THE AGES)*

Notice the light construction of Spanish field pieces. Spain did not use threaded bolts. They hammered down the ends of smooth bolts over washers.[3] Unlike the British, they used Δ headed nails.[4] What is missing (in the drawing) are high wheel chocks which were behind the wheels to prevent violent recoils. I have seen such cannon leap a foot in the air. Most cannon in the Alamo were Spanish field artillery.

In movies we see cannons fire and the tube doesn't even wiggle. In real life, recoil was a big problem. Gunners at the Alamo had to give this a great deal of thought. An unanchored cannon will, when fired, leap back into anyone standing there. Broken bones tend to slow down gunners.

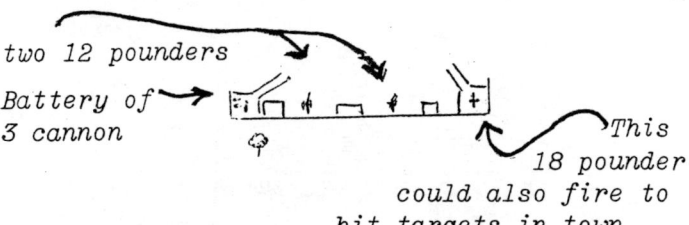

POSITION #3
The west wall

This wall faced San Antonio. Number 9 was the largest artillery piece between the Mississippi and Rio Grande: an 18 pounder. There wasn't a place inside San Antonio this cannon couldn't reach. #10 was a 12 pounder. #11 usually pointed west but could turn north. Notice the semi-circle of stakes outside the wall. With the west wall being the lowest of the main plaza walls these devices were made to slow down attackers.

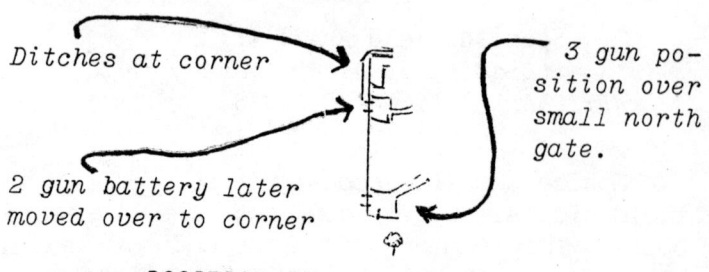

Ditches at corner

3 gun position over small north gate.

2 gun battery later moved over to corner

POSITION #4

The north wall

The North wall was defended by batteries on the corners. While one piece was being fired the other could be loaded. These might have been 12 pounders. #11,12,13 were on top of a wooden platform built over a small north gate. This was a secondary gate and not part of the original plans of the mission.

All the artillery on this north wall was probably on siege mounts and probably utilized ropes stretched across wall corners as recoil anchors.

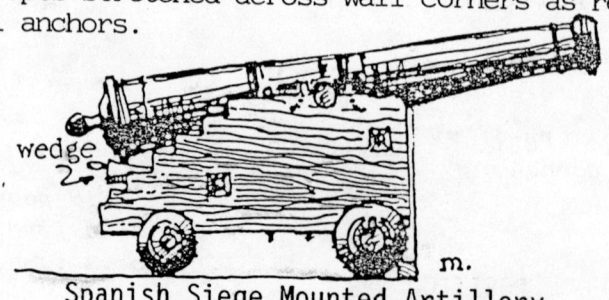

Spanish Siege Mounted Artillery
=Albert Manucy

The advantage of these mounts was their low profile and ease of construction. The big weakness was in difficulty of it to allow the cannon barrel to aim down at a steep angle. Anyone close to a wall defended by guns thus mounted was safe from them because they couldn't aim downwards.

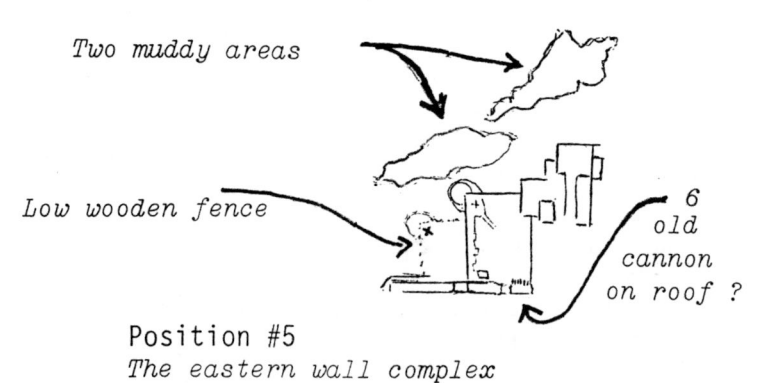

Two muddy areas

Low wooden fence

6 old cannon on roof ?

Position #5
The eastern wall complex

This side seems weak but the barrier of outer walls was a deterrent. And once a force pierced them they would face the higher walls of the Long and High Barracks. Meantime, defenders could fire down at the attackers trapped between the walls like fish in a bowl.

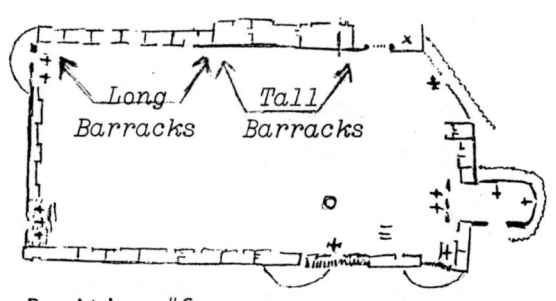

Long Barracks *Tall Barracks*

Position #6
The Long and Tall Barracks

This position was the strongest in the Alamo. Especially the two-story part. Some have claimed the lower rooms of these buildings were not connected. But Capt. Navarro shows they were connected and he had been inside them on barracks inspections.

Map A, drawn on March 3, shows 6 lines pointing east from the two-story barracks. I have puzzled over those lines and come to the conclusion they were 6 older Spanish cannon (which usually featured 8-9 foot barrels) but were of small caliber. There would have been a number of very old pieces in the mission because Spanish frontier posts tended to accumulate all the old 'junk' artillery no one else wanted. By placing these old pieces on the high roof the defenders could make an attack from the east more costly. But because they were on siege mounts and so difficult to reload (i.e. the very long, narrow barrels), they could not be depressed and aimed at targets within the plaza, once the outer walls had been stormed.

Early Spanish Cannon

Probably left-overs from the old Presidio fort near the mission which was abandoned according to Morfi. [5]

What other proof exists that the 6 lines on Map A, were indeed old cannon barrels ? A comment from a witness during the final assault indicates massed artillery fire briefly from this area. These old tubes must served as one-shot affairs, with no reloading.

NOTES

1. P.94, Friar Morfi, HISTORY OF TEXAS : 1673-1779.
2. P.92, Hanighan, Frank, SANTA ANNA.
3. P.50, Manucy, Albert, ARTILLERY THROUGH THE AGES.
4. P.55, Ibid.
5. Pp.224-225, Friar Morfi, HISTORY OF TEXAS : 1673-1779.

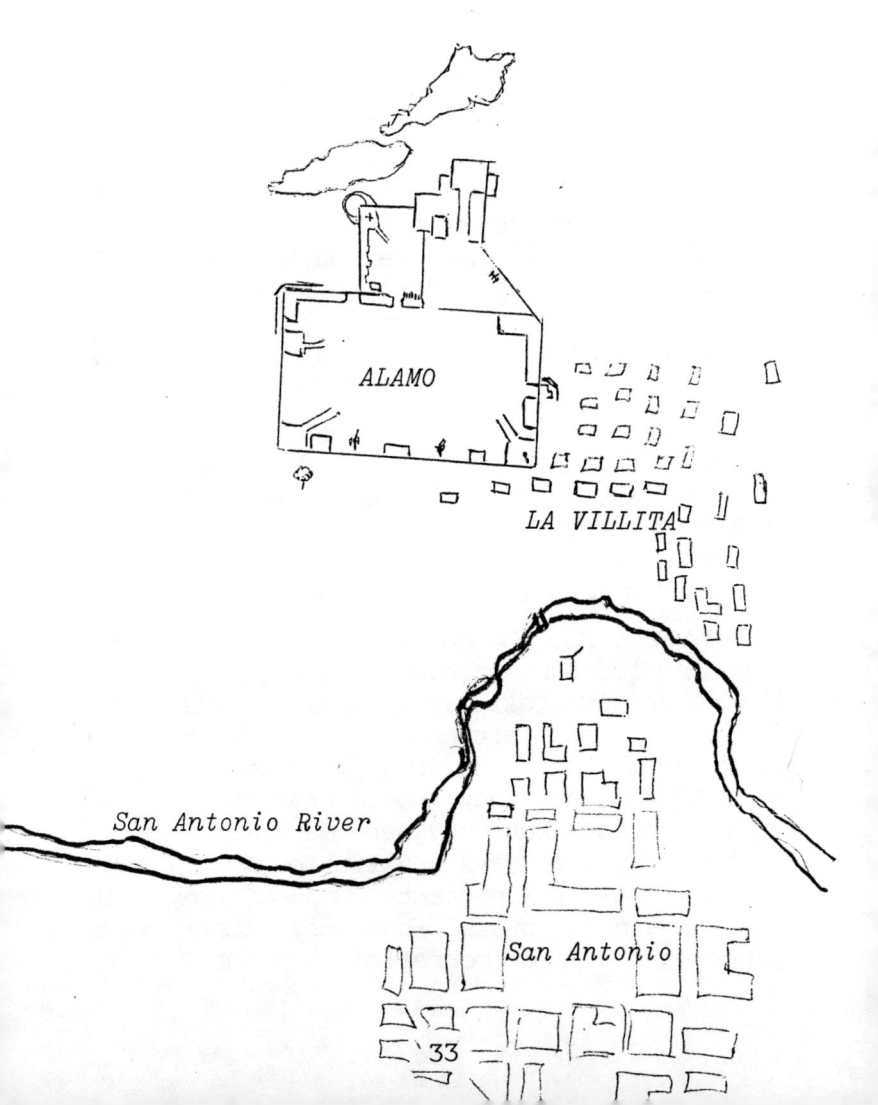

THE DICTATOR'S FIRST BRIGADE ARRIVES

On December 25, 1835, at San Luis Potosi the Dictator reviewed his army. 6,000 troops. The best army Mexico had ever placed in the field. All those years of military experience and love of Napoleon had paid off. A loan of 450 million pesos (about 7½ million dollars) and healthy Catholic church contributions had given the Napoleon of the west a well equipped army with 1,500 cavalry, 4,500 infantry, and 21 artillery pieces.

There were good and bad units in this army. By this I mean the amount of military experience. The Reserve units can be divided into 2 categories: the trained and untrained. It was all drill. But don't dismiss this activity as mere parade ground antics. Musket armed troops had to be able to maneuver. Without drill they were a armed mob.

On Nov. 17, he sent his pet, Gen. Sesma, to aid Cos in San Antonio. He was expected to move quickly. Some fellow officers claimed he didn't *want* to get to San Antonio quickly.[1] It would be Dec. 26, when Sesma met the defeated elements of Cos's forces at Laredo.

By Dec. 22, the entire First Brigade was marching for San Antonio. Two days later the Second Brigade followed. Last of all, the Cavalry Brigade left on Dec. 26. They made up over one-sixth of the army [2] and on the open plains of Texas they could have been a decisive factor. But they were marching in the winter. Winter grass has little food value but this wasn't important because how could the animals eat grass when they either were carrying riders or corralled at night ?

First Division
  First Brigade
  (Gen. Sesma)

1 Matamoros Inf.
1A   "   Chasseurs
2 Jemenez Inf.
2A   "   Chasseurs
3 San Luis Potosi Inf.
3A   "   Chasseurs
4 Dolores Cavalry Regt.
5 Artillery (8 pieces)
6 Allende Inf.
6A Tampico Cavalry Regt.

Second Division
  Second Brigade
  (Gen. Gaona)

7 Zapadores Sappers
8 Aldama Inf.
8A   "   Chasseurs
9 Toluca Inf.
9A   "   Chasseurs
10 Queretaro Inf.
10A   "   Chasseurs
11 Guanajuato Inf.
11A   "   Chasseurs
12 Artillery (6 pieces)

Third Brigade
(part of 2nd Div.)

13 Guerrero Inf.
13A   "   Chasseurs
14 First Active - Mexico City
14A   "   Chasseurs
15 Guadalajara Inf.
15A   "   Chasseurs
16 Tres Villas Inf.
16A   "   Chasseurs
17 Artillery (6 pieces)

MEXICAN ARMY AT BEGINNING OF CAMPAIGN

Why were they marching in winter ? Let the Napoleon of the west tell us:

"If the only 4 favorable months of the year were not taken advantage of, the army, in the midst of the hardships of a campaign, would perish of hunger and of the effects of the climate..."[3]

He says this to justify a march *in the winter* ! Are the only favorable months of the year the winter months ? Then he tells us the real reason for this rush to get to San Antonio:

"... it was of the utmost importance to prevent the enemy from strenghtening its position or receiving reenforcements..."[4]

San Antonio was the capitol of the provence, the largest all-Mexican town there, and he wanted it for his base of operations for this campaign.

"Bexar was held by the enemy and it was necessary to open the door to our future operations by taking it."[5]

Then there was the Alamo which had been captured from Cos. Once he arrived and saw it was occupied he realized:

"An assault would infuse our soldiers with that enthusiam of the first triumph that would make them superior in the future to those of the enemy."[6]

In other words, he planned to use it as a example to show his soldiers how easily the Texas rebels could be beaten.

A priest on the Medina River gave them the strength of the Americans in San Antonio. The Dictator then decided to send a *fast* striking force of cavalry to capture the rebels in San Antonio. Who did he choose for an operation requiring speed and deciveness ? Why, his pet : Sesma.

Gen. Sesma rode out. Was spotted by Dr. Sutherland and then set up a defensive position because he expected to be *attacked*. He was still waiting for the attack when the Dictator and the rest of the First Brigade arrived. The Dictator would later say:

"...the surprise I had ordered to be carried out would have saved the time consumed and the blood shed later in the taking of the Alamo."[7]

The Americans were warned by Dr. Sutherland and had time to withdraw into the Alamo. A flag was on the church steeple. A Mexican officer saw it from a distance and remembered it was a Mexican flag *with 2 white stars.*[8] The stars stood for the two provinces of Coahuila and Texas. That flag was taken down and used at the Alamo.

Now that we have mentioned this flag it is time to discuss what flags were used in the Alamo. Travis, in his letters, says 'our flag' (one). But the flag sent to Mexico by the Dictator was the company flag of the New Orleans Grays. Some writers are claiming this *company* flag was 'the flag' of which Travis spoke. Wrong. A small company flag would have been posted at the headquarters of the commander of that company. In other words, that Company flag would have been on a pole over the building where Bowie lay. The building at the south gate: the Low Barracks.

Remember, Travis and Bowie were joint commanders when the 2 starred flag was lowered when the Mexicans arrived. If *that* was the flag they had flown in San Antonio, then it is only logical those same two commanders would place that same flag over the Alamo as their main flag. But as we shall see, I think Travis would later alter this flag somewhat.

Remember that Texas had not yet declared independence. Remember that at least Bowie, with his knowledge of Mexican politics, would realize the value of that flag. It reminded all who saw it that the Dictator was depriving those two provinces of their rights under the 1824 Constitution. Indeed, Gen. Almonte in his diary tells us what those two stars signified.[9] If he knew, then so did every one else in the Mexican army.

There is something curious about Map A. It shows locations for three (3) commanders in the Alamo. How would an Engineer, making that map, arrive at such a conclusion ? And isn't it strange that he correctly shows where Bowie and Travis had made their headquarters ? Bowie with the Grays flag to the right of the south gate and Travis with the 2 starred flag above his room midway of the west wall. And...wait a minute! Yet another Commander is shown residing in the middle room of the chapel on the north side. The very room where Dickinson and his wife lived during the seige. So there must have been a *third* flag above that room and I think I know what it was. Captain Dickinson was in command of the artillery in the chapel. He had also been in command of the Gonzales cannon in the first battle of the rebellion - the 'Come And Get It' fight when Cos had sent a force to retake a cannon the settlers were using for local defense against Indians. The flag the rebels had used was white with the drawing of a cannon. Above the drawing the words: 'Come and Take it.'

A witness would later remember that after that cannon was buried (on the way to San Antonio to attack Cos) he last saw that flag "leaning against a tree."[10] He guessed that it might have been forgotten and left behind. [11] But the Captain of an artillery unit is the one most likely to value his unit's flag. I suspect Dickinson not only saved it but was flying it over his quarters in the chapel when Map A was drawn.

These three Alamo flags give a new dimension to the struggle. The Dictator most assurely would not have sent the main flag to Mexico City because it would have reminded too many of the violation of that 1824 Constitution. And he would not have sent the home made "Come And Get It" flag because it was too crude and defiant. But that finely made little company flag of the Grays? That was another matter. It was his 'proof' that volunteers from the U.S. were aiding the rebels.

I noticed the Dictator chooses 600 as the number of the Alamo garrison. 600 is about 3 companies. If challenged by political opponates on this 600 figure, he could then have said, " They had a flag for each company." 19th Century Dictators used lies as adroitly as Russian dictators do today.

In the Alamo were about 90± Grays, 30 colonists from Travis' Regular Army, Crockett was joined by 3 more in Texas including Capt. Harrison, leader (on paper) of his tiny unit. And 50-60 wounded from the December fight in San Antonio. These are the forgotten men and everyone overlooks them.

Dr. Sutherland saw them:

"The combined forces at Bexar now numbered 172, but of these some 25 or 30 were on the sick list..." [12]

Mrs Dickinson, in her statement in 1875, takes special care to mention these men near the beginning of her testimony:

"Among the beseiged were 50-60 wounded men from Cos's fight." [13]

She and Sutherland ought to know - they were there. And since Sutherland left soon after the Mexicans arrived on the first day - before any shooting took place - he cannot be talking about casualties occurring during the seige. Yet Walter Lord, Tinkle, Myers, and Potter pretend these wounded men never existed. Why didn't Travis mention these men in his letters from the Alamo ? Notice that Travis, in letter after letter makes the point, "We have not yet lost a man." Now suppose he had added "...but we have 50-60 wounded who were here earlier from another battle." That confuses matters. Lawyer Travis needed it as black and white as he could make it. To say "We have not lost a man" was to the point and truthful.

Who looked after the wounded ? Dr. Sutherland says Dr. Pollard was the 'surgeon of the command."[14] Naturally, he would have seen after them. There is a probabilty 3 wounded died during the seige from December wounds. Three bodies in frontier clothes were found years later under the debris in the chapel.[15] Death by gangrene could account for them.

This large number of wounded could also be one more reason Travis <u>stayed and fought.</u> Notice that Travis' letters never mention that Bowie is bedridden. If he *had* mentioned it then we could question why no mention of the other wounded.

Where were the wounded housed in the Alamo ? At least before the Mexican army came there would have been food and attention provided by Mexican women from La Villita near the south gate. This was a cluster of buildings which had accumulated during the years to allow easier contact between locals and garrison soldiers living in the Alamo.

By housing the wounded in the Low Barrack building at the south gate these men could be easily reached by those caring for them. Another clue is Capt. Navarro's remembering there were a large number of kitchen utensils in one of the south gate rooms. Cooking food for the entire garrison in a place near those who were badly wounded was logical. The fact that Bowie was lodged here would support this theory. I suspect the wounded were later moved to scattered, fixed positions where their use of pre-loaded muskets could aid in defending the Alamo.

NOTES

1. P.15, Pena, WITH SANTA ANNA IN TEXAS.
2. P.20, Ibid.
3. P.12, Castaneda, THE MEXICAN SIDE OF THE TEXAN REVOLUTION.
4. Ibid.
5. Ibid.
6. P.13, Ibid.
7. P.12, Ibid.
8. Feb.23 entry in Almonte's diary.
9. Ibid.
10. P.42, as told by S.R. Bostick, DeShields, TALL MEN WITH LONG RIFLES.
11. Ibid.
12. P.137, DeShields, TALL MEN WITH LONG...
13. John Ford Papers, "Testimony of Mrs Hanning touching on the Alamo Massacre."
14. P.137, DeShields, TALL MEN WITH LONG RIFLES
15. P.15, Marick, Mary, MEMOIRS OF MARY A. ...

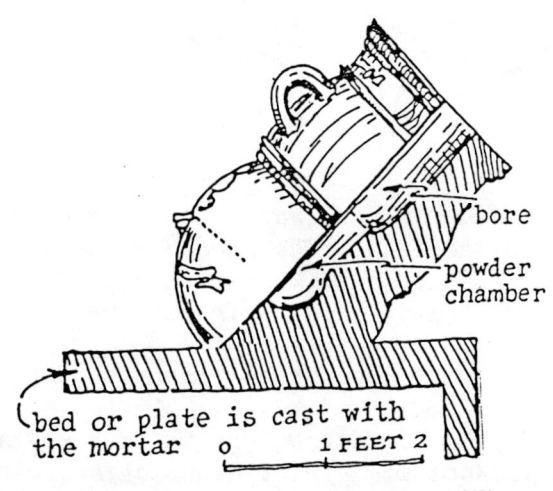

SPANISH 5-INCH BRONZE MORTAR (1788).

REGULAR MEXICAN INFANTRY *from an enlarged detail of a contemporary painting. This is a 12 man squad with 3 drummers and 1 fifer in front. They have tight white trousers & blue coats with white crossed belts. Even in a squad the commander walks in middle - front. Exactly where the Commander of Battalion sized formations was supposed to be.*

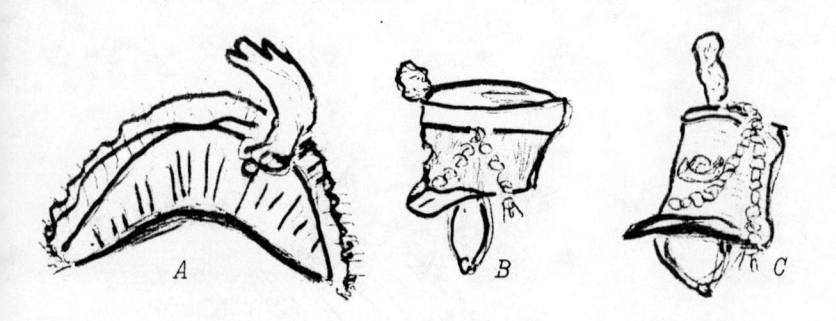

A. Officer's hat. *Worn with a pointed end to the front. The larger - the better.*
B. Grenadier hat. *Worn with red pompom and red braid. Only their hats were wide-topped.*
C. Cuzadore Hat. *Green pompom and braid.*

Regular infantry wore white pompoms and Santa Anna was strict about chin straps being fastened. Some units had great-coats & wore them over their regular coats depending on the weather.

THE SEIGE

March 23

The Seige Begins

Around 1 o'clock a sentry in the church tower saw Mexican cavalry. Dr. Sutherland and Smith rode out and confirmed the report. The Americans moved into the Alamo across a foot-bridge and a fording place on the river separating the town from the mission.

At 3 P.M. Mexican skirmishers entered the town from the west and fanned out, going from house to house and street to street with guns ready. Behind them came the infantry. Behind these moved blocks of cavalry ready to advance toward any gunfire.

In the afternoon the Mexicans set up a battery of cannon and a mortar near the river and fired 4 grenades with the latter.

A horseman came from the Alamo and met Gen. Almonte (head of staff) at the river. It was Jameson with a note from Bowie. Almonte told him their only chance was to simply surrender and depend on the mercy of the Dictator. Jameson was followed up by Martin with a note from Travis. Basically the same message - asking for terms and delaying for more time to prepare defenses.

There was no more firing from the Mexican side this day. The rest of the Dictator's staff arrived. Among them his secretary: Caro who saw the old mission and wasn't impressed.

"...*a mere corral and nothing more.*"[1]

In the Alamo the men were excited. No danger of being bored now ! The 2 different messengers tells us that Travis and Bowie were each showing their 'rank' to each other. But Bowie has only a few hours now before being bedridden. Whatever it was remains a mystery. Dr. Sutherland examined him , saying Bowie was injured while passing under a cannon and suffered broken ribs. But then he adds that:

"...Bowie, whose disease being of a peculiar nature, was not to be cured by an ordinary treatment." [2]

A curious choice of words. But the detail he uses in describing Bowies injury has usually been disreguarded by historians. Remember, Bowie would have told the doctor how his illness came about. Why not believe him ?

Tonight he and Travis and the other officers would make defensive plans. Bowie earlier to Governor Smith on the 'Conception' battle, described the same strategy used later at the Alamo. Whether that 'Conception' report was actually composed by Bowie or by Fannin who was his co-commander in that fight (and had 2 years of West Point) is not important. What is important is Bowie's understanding of the concept of dividing defensive forces while keeping a reserve. This is part of Bowie's report:

"...When the fog rose it was apparent to all that we were surrounded...preparation was made by extending our right flank... to the south, and placing the second division on the left, on the same side; so that they might be prepared for the enemy should they charge into the angle, and avoid the effect of a cross fire of our own men, and likewise form a compact body, so that either might reinforce the other at the shortest notice without crossing

the angle - an exposed ground..."[3]

   This division of the Alamo defenders so that they could reinforce each other is very important. Travis by himself probably would not have thought of it. So we must give Bowie credit for the Alamo's basic defensive concept.

   The overall plan of defense seems to have been:
A. Assign units of men to specific areas of the mission.
B. When necessary, shift these units to reinforce each other.
C. The 2 main open areas (Plaza and area in front of Chapel) were to become 'killing zones' if the Mexicans got inside outer walls.
D. Keep on the offensive to stall a final assault.

February 24, Wednesday

A Small Test Of The Alamo Defenses

   In the morning it becomes known to everyone in the Alamo that Bowie has given total command to Travis. Where were the men assigned ? Crockett's party was given the wooden wall between the Chapel and Low Barracks. Dickinson was given enough Gonzales men to operate the 4 cannon in the Chapel plus most if not all the boys to serve as 'powder monkies'. They would carry already-measured powder charges from the main magazine to the other cannon in the fort.

   At 9 A.M. the Dictator distributed merchendise he stole from Smith's store in San Antonio. At 11 A.M. he rode out with his staff to study the Alamo from all sides. He also started his men working on a new battery

45

west of the Alamo some 350 yds. away. A 5 in. mortar and two 9 pounders were in it. These guns opened fire at the 2 Alamo cannon on the west wall.

The 9 pounders had come from England and were very accurate. By dusk both Alamo cannon had been dismounted. The mortars had also hit a horse in the corral with shrapnel.

This counter-battery firing was simple Napoleonic tactics:
> *"First, silence the guns of the work by a powerful artillery fire."*
> *- Jomini* [4]

But it made the Dictator more confident. At this time he had the Matamoros, Jimenez, and San Luis Potosi Battalions with the excellent Dolores Cavalry Regiment. This was the entire First Brigade.

At the same time his cannon began firing he moved some skirmishers from the San Luis Battalion toward a cluster of houses called La Villita near the southwest corner of the Alamo. This would have been a company of that Battalion's light infantry (called 'Cuzadores' and armed with Baker rifled muskets[5]). About 150-180 men.

Secretary Caro was among those watching. He tells us what happened:

> *"Santa Anna placed a battery of 2 cannon and a mortar 600 paces from the fort, and began firing, taking position at the same time of several small houses to the left. These were nearer to the enemies position and our troops had several killed and wounded in the operation. Around the fortress there were ditches used by the enemy to fire upon our troops."* [6]

He was watching from the safe side of the river so he could not see how many casualies there were. It had been a test that probably saw Crockett's riflemen being shifted to the area to support the musket firing defenders.

As night came the Dictator had some decisions to make. He had tested the defenses by moving closer in the La Villita area, obviously trying to save men by using the houses for cover. He now decided to launch a larger attack the next day with the light companies of the 2 untried battalions. With the option to send in regular infantry.

Among the Mexicans evacuated from La Villita was a very beautiful girl whose mother made it clear would have to be married to the Dictator before he could have her. The Dictator found a man tonight willing to pose as a priest. Officers were told of the hoax. Dictators must have their fun.

Colonel Bringas was sent near midnight to cross the river and scout La Villita. But as the Colonel was crossing with his men they were fired on from the Alamo. The Colonel fell in the water and one of his men killed before they ran. The other side of the river was still clearly controlled by the Alamo.

Some local Mexicans visited the Alamo tonight to see their relatives. A Mexican boy remembered being pulled up into the Chapel window and across a cannon positioned there.[7] Potter thinks this window was on the south or east side of the Chapel.[8] But there were no windows on *those* walls. He would have gone in the window to the left of the big doorway. A small cannon here could enfilade Crockett's wooden wall. A cannon most assurely would *not* have been emplaced in the window to the right because the field of fire was too narrow.

Little details like this reveal how shrewdly the defenders were placing their artillery.

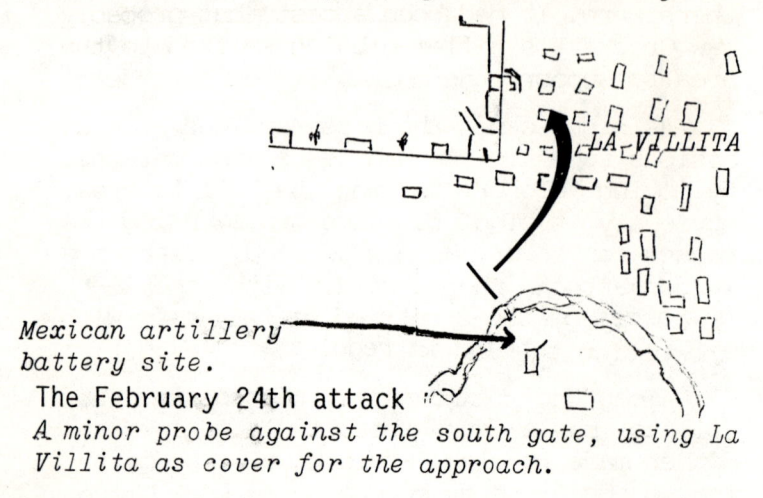

Mexican artillery battery site.

The February 24th attack
A minor probe against the south gate, using La Villita as cover for the approach.

FEBRUARY 25, Thursday

    A Major Assault Fails

Very early in the morning the 1st Mexican battery of two 9 pounders began firing. A new battery further north had been emplaced just across the river. Soon those two 9 pounders were also firing.

At 10 o'clock the light companies of the Matamoros and Jimenez advanced towards La Villita. Behind them on the west side of the river the rest of the army waited. Some Alamo men ran into La Villita with torches. As the fighting grew fierce the Dictator committed the entire Matamoros and Jeminez Battalions with a column of mounted chasseurs.[9] Lt. Col. Pena would later say only the Matamoros were advanced. But Almonte says *both* and Almonte was in a better position as Staff Officer to know. The San Luis Battalion was in reserve.

But more Mexicans only made more targets. The small 4 pounders at the south gate kept a steady stream of shrapnel flying each time a charge on the gate was attempted. And on the walls Crockett's men completely outclassed the Baker rifled muskets used by the Cuzadore companies. Their white, crossed belts must have made excellent aiming points. In frontier shooting matches charcoal 'X's were used with shooters aiming for the center.

At noon the two Battalions pulled back to the river in confusion. It was definitely *not* a planned, orderly withdrawal.[10] It had been a shooting gallery in La Villita. Being so close to American rifles was not healthy. In two hours Crockett's party alone could have fired some 1200 rounds with 40 minutes for rest periods. Crockett had been given 25 lbs. of excellent Du Pont rifle powder by the Whigs of Philadelphia in 1835. That powder was being used by his group to good effect. The Ole' Fox himself could have fired 80 rounds in this attack. And how many of those 80 would have been misses?

The speed of the small caliber rifle balls made a more deadly wound according to the theories of the time. A German engineer who had been in Santa Anna's army in 1833-34 explains the theory:

"...the actual advantage of this rifle was the small size of the ball. It is more deadly because the opening of the wound is so small that the blood cannot flow out of the wound, so it flows into the interior of the body. Thus, the smallest wound becomes fatal." [11]

One thing about these early rifles we tend to overlook: the 'crack' sound occurring after they fired meant the ball had broken the sound barrier. A human target was struck *before* he heard the rifle which had fired at him. This gave no opportunity to duck at the sound of the gun.

The Dictator was furious. He wanted to take the Alamo today so he could quickly advance into Texas and hang the leaders of this silly revolt. He again called for Colonel Bringas. He told him to ride west and tell General Gaona to rush forward the Aldama, Toluca, and Zappadore Battalions. The three best battalions in the entire Mexican Army.

Some writers have said he asked for the 3 best *'companies'*.[12] And yes, this is what the Dictator later wrote. But as we shall see, he ordered Battalions - not companies. A company was 180 men. A Battalion was six companies !

That night the Dictator sent Col. Morales to oversee the digging of trenches in La Villita. He had decided to hold that position with trenches. Notice he has them dug during the night.

He also has two more batteries emplaced. One about 300 yards south of the Alamo and one near the powderhouse 1,000 yards to the southeast. Both batteries were to be supported by the Matamoros Battalion which moved up in the night to dig trenches linking the two positions.

Now a seige with trenches would begin. He would have to wait for reinforcements to try another storming. The north side of the Alamo had been tested in the afternoon but cannon and musket fire had driven off the small group of Mexicans. And the east wall was approached too closely by a group of Dolores cavalrymen. A party of Grays ran out the north gate, slipped around the northeast corner and let them have a few volleys. The horsemen quickly rode off.

This would be an eventful night. Seguin and another Mexican rode through a screen of cavalry after boldly ridding up to them. He was carrying letters from Travis for Gov. Smith and Fannin. After Seguin had left, nine men from the Alamo came to the N.W. trenches where troops were emplacing more cannon.[13] These Alamo deserters were local Mexicans, with perhaps a Anglo friend or two, recruited by Seguin. The fighting today and the departure of their leader was too much. *Don't forget these men*. We are going to come back to them later to clear up one of the Alamo's controversies. But right now it is important for us to remember that these '9' men have walked right up to the Mexicans and asked to see the Dictator.[14] Would Texan rebels have dared ? No.

On this night the Dictator went through his phony marriage (he was already married). Travis sent parties to tear down abandoned La Villita houses and drag the wood back to use for firewood, cooking, and beacons. This last item was extremely important. One thing which must have haunted Travis was fear of a night attack with Mexicans coming over the walls in the darkness with no one being able to see to fire at them.

It is good he read 'SCOTTISH CHIEFS.' There is a situation in the book when a night attack is made on a castle and it is important to kill the guards around a beacon to smother the flames.[15] The lighting of these beacons on the morning of the 6th will explain a strange scene witnessed by Col. Pena.

Yes, this has been a busy day and night. The Alamo was proving more difficult to take

51

than anyone had thought possible. The Dictator has already lost *at least* 200 men.

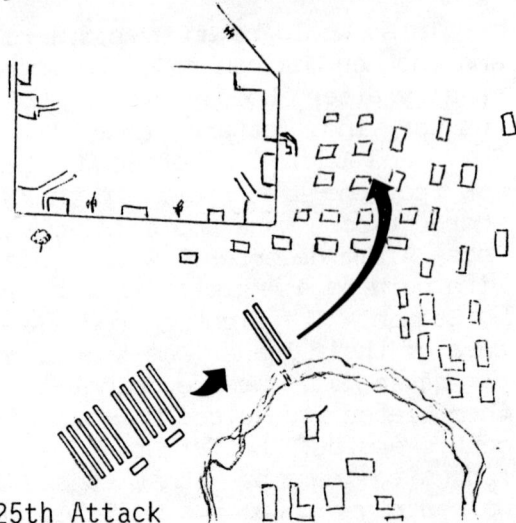

The February 25th Attack
A major attempt to storm the Alamo by attacking in force through La Villita with the main gate being the focal point of the attack.

FEBRUARY 26, Friday

The Elimination Of La Villita

A northern wind blew very strong this morning. It was 39 degrees but after the sun rose it reached 60.

Dawn saw a group of Dolores cavalry again circling close to the eastern walls of the Alamo. Again a party of Grays ran out the north gate and gave them the same treatment as yesterday. Was this a ploy by Travis ? Why didn't he simply order the cannons on the east walls to fire ? Or did he suspect that they wanted him to fire the cannons and waste powder ? I think artillerymen had been ordered to save their powder for big infantry attacks. Let the taunting, darting cavalry flit about - but don't waste powder on them !

Travis sent a squad into La Villita to pull in more wood. Another squad went north to skirmish with the Mexicans in the new battery on the east side of the river.

On this day Fannin left Goliad in the afternoon with 320 men and 4 cannon. 200 *yards* later they camped for the night after a wagon axle broke. This incident tells us all we need to know about Mr. Fannin. He could now say he tried to reach the Alamo. Fannin had told Gov. Smith in a letter that he was not capable of commanding.[16] Looking back at the 'Conception' fight where he and Bowie had each commanded a company it is easy to see now that it had been Bowie who made the decisions and carried them out. Fannin alone could neither make nor carry out a decision. He would later pay with his life and those of the over 400 men he led.

About 7 P.M. the Dictator sent a Mexican engineer across the river to examine something about the Alamo. He was soon picked off by a rifleman. We can imagine the entire army watching from around their campfires as the figure went closer...closer and then a single 'crack' from a long barreled gun and he falls as all had expected. Was the Dictator bored and needing some excitement ? The man on the other end of that rifle could very well have been Crockett. We can imagine, as the Mexican approached, someone yelling, "Here's one for you, Crockett."

Night. Another party raided La Villita, burning huts and hauling in wood. The San Luis Potosi Battalion was now in trenches which passed through what was left of the place. After tonight the area between their trenches and the Alamo would be free of obstacles, giving a clear field of fire across the smoking rubble.

Tonight the Mexicans made bugle calls and shouted to make the defenders restless.

FEBRUARY 27, Saturday
Digging In

A cold north wind was strong at dawn and would continue all day and night with a high of 39. (*Note: all this daily weather data is from Gen. Almonte's journal*)

The Mexicans blocked the irrigation ditch leading to the Alamo. Jameson then had the old well in the plaza dug out. Water was important not just for drinking but for making little moats around certain areas.

Almonte remembers on this day, "Enemy worked hard to repair some entrenchments." [17]

They were making a trench outside the north wall. A moat or trench would also be dug in an semi-circle around the exposed cannon at the eastern corral.

In the mid afternoon the Dictator rode around his lines with a glittering group of aids and Dragoons. He wanted to see what the rebels were doing. At 2 P.M. today the Gonzales men left to reinforce the Alamo. Tonight Bonham left for Goliad to ask Fannin again for help. Travis should have saved good paper.

FEBRUARY 28, Sunday
Rumors Of Fannin

It was 40 degrees at 7 A.M. The day would be overcast with a light rain.

The Mexicans began working on new battery positions in front of the old mill which was southeast of the Alamo. At this point let me say that in my opinion all this building of new cannon emplacements - when he had only 8 nine pounders and 2 mortars on hand, makes me skeptical whether most positions were ever even *used* to fire at the Alamo.

It seems to me he was trying to confuse the defenders as to the *direction* of his next attack. Any daylight assault would have to be preceeded by artillery fire *from the direction of the attack*. By continually digging new emplacements he was making them waste energy preparing for attacks from all directions. And if so, it backfired on the Dictator because the final assault would find the defenders ready for attacks from any direction.

Besides, each iron 9 pound cannon ball shot at the Alamo was retrieved and saved to be fired right back later with the numberous 12 pounders in the mission. An even better combination was to fire *two* 9 pound balls in a 12 pounder. This load would be tested on March 1, with very good results.

As the Dictator added to the defender's stock of cannon balls they also prepared home made loads of scrap iron to use at close range. Spanish cannister shot was made of brass balls and evidently Cos had fired all his cannister shells. We know he used cannister extensively in the December street fighting for San Antonio. [18]

At 7 A.M. today a messanger brought news from spies that Fannin was marching to the Alamo. Later today a young Gonzales Texan named Ben Highsmith rode up Powder House Hill as he tried to reach the Alamo. But some Dolores Cavalrymen chased him 6 miles before they gave up.

Meanwhile, the cannonading of the mission by 9 pounders continued. These guns were too light to be used as seige artillery. With the outer walls 30 inches thick and made of adobe mud and stone, there was no chance of breaking down the walls at the 300 yd. range (and more) of the present batteries.

This rainy Sunday ended with the Dictator worried that this seige was becoming more of a problem than he'd thought. Now he had to find units to intercept Fannin.

Tonight a Mexican sentry was knifed. It might have happened as he was about to discover a spy going to the Alamo to tell Travis that Fannin was coming.

FEBRUARY 29, Monday
The Mystery Battalion Arrives

It was warm again. Temperature rose to 55 but tonight the wind would begin blowing hard from the west.

Today the Allende Battalion arrived and took up positions on the east side of the Alamo. It was made up of drafted men from the provence of Zacatecas. This was the provence the Dictator had crushed the previous year when they rebelled against him.

New Orleans newspapers would report that a unit from Zacatecas had arrived 'in chains.' Convict companies were used in Mexican armies since most convicts were political prisoners. In fact, the last reinforcements for Cos had been 500 convicts in chains.[19] That this

Allende unit had a number of men in chains could very well be true. Perhaps they were former rebel soldiers.

First this unit was assigned the eastern side of the Alamo. Then, at midnight, they were marched toward Goliad to intercept Fannin. The officer chosen to lead this expedition ? Right. Gen. Sesma. The other officers must have jumped with anger. "He gets to do everything !" many must have muttered.

With Sesma went the excellent Dolores cavalry regiment. Replacing them at the Alamo was the Tampico Regiment which had arrived as an escort to the Allende Battalion. Why move them at night ? To prevent the Alamo from knowing about it and perhaps warning Fannin.

General Castrillon was then ordered to stretch the Matamoros and Jimenez units to fill the gap when the unit left at midnight. This line ran from the Powder House to the irrigation ditch - 800 yards northeast of the Alamo.

Before Sesma left tonight, the Dictator called him over and reminded him, "In this war, you know, there ought to be no prisoners."20 It was midnight and the west wind now shifted and blew from the north.

On this day Bonham arrived at Goliad. And just as the Dictator had earlier sent an Engineer to his death, so it was that at 7:30 P.M. today the Dictator now sent a Private named Secundino Alvarez to examine something south of the Alamo. He was a member of the San Luis Battalion : the Battalion stationed in the trenches across La Villita near the south gate. It might have been entertainment for the Dictator but it was death for Secundino.

MARCH 1, Tuesday

The Gonzales Men Arrive

It was 36 degrees in the morning. A clear day with no wind.

At 3 A.M. in the morning 32 Gonzales men arrived at the south gate. They had passed through the thinned east line where the Allende unit had been.

The Dictator rode over to the Mill site and gave Castrillon a lecture on how to stop people from riding to and from the Alamo. While there, he ordered his artillery Comamder, Ampudia, to dig more gun emplacements.

This afternoon the 12 pounder in the center of the west wall fired two 9 pound balls at a house on the main plaza. One missed but the other hit the Dictator's headquarters. They were testing double-shot loads.

The arrival of 32 more riflemen meant a second reserve unit. But their assigned area was the roof of the 2 story barracks. It was ideal for riflemen. Once the outer walls had fallen, rifles on that roof could hit everything in the Alamo plaza.

Morale was high in the mission. Crockett had his fiddle and McGregor his bagpipe. Mrs. Dickinson remembered that he had some favorite tunes but she doesn't name them.

At Washington-On-The-Brazos the delegates met today to form a new government for Texas.

MARCH 2, Wednesday

Where Is Fannin ?

A cold 34 degrees all day. But no wind.

An artillery bombardment continued to add

more 9 pound balls to the Alamo's supply. Fannin was expected today and the sentries on the walls must have watched carefully for any sign of increased activity among the Mexican forces on the eastern side.

There was activity around the Dictator's headquarters all day. General Cos and Captain Navarro arrived ahead of the three elite Battalions. Cos wanted revenge for his defeat 2 months ago. Navarro wanted revenge for the humiliation of having to sign that surrender. Both conviently overlooked their promises at that time not to enter Texas again.

A cavalryman, Trinidad Delgado, attached to the San Luis Battalion, drowned when his horse threw him into the river south of La Villita. It was a cold day to drown. This event also tells us the river between the town and Mission was deep and dangerous.

On this day Urrea destroyed Dr. Grant's force with a ambush. Many of Grant's men tried to surrender. They were killed anyway. We should not feel sorry for Grant. He was on a personal wild goose chase to retake property he owned near Matamoros. The tragedy is that over 100 of his men had been enticed away from the original Alamo garrison. These men were needed at the Alamo where they would have made a difference. Now their unburied bodies would feed the vultures.

The day ends with the Alamo men asking over and over, "Where is that damned Fannin ?" The Mexicans were also waiting. Waiting for the reinforcements they needed to storm the Alamo. *(Note: Fannin was expected on this day because they all thought he had left Goliad the 29th - so he should have reached them on March 2nd)*

MARCH 3, Thursday
Travis' Finest Hour

It was a clear day. 40 degrees and no wind.

At 11 A.M. Bonham rode back into the Alamo. We wonder what punishment the Dictator issued to the Mexicans supposed to be watching on that side. Bonham brought news all right. News only for Travis's ear. Bonham was the ideal southern gentleman and what he had to say was for the commander only : *Fannin was definitely not coming*. Travis told him not to repeat this news to anyone. The decision was now that of Travis. Either give up the Alamo or fight it out to the end with the few men he had.

Probably any other man would have seriously considered the former but not the man who wrote in his diary "Today I turned back for the first time in my life." There would be no turning back. Travis kept to himself in the Alamo. We know this because Millsaps' letter to his wife states this fact.[21] He did not mix well anyway. Romantics are usually loners. He would have thought of Rebecca Cummings and the good times they'd had. He would have looked at the lock of hair she gave him, probably now in a locket about his neck. He would eventually tell the men what Bonham had said. But not until Saturday. This afternoon he would lie to them. Ask them to hold out a little longer. Say that help was coming soon.

I realize the above sounds like something from a novel but when we reach Saturday I shall present enough arguments to convince you that A. Travis knew *on the 3rd* there would be no aid. B. That at the meeting held on the 3rd he would with - hold this news.

C. On Saturday he would *admit* to them that he had with-held this news.

About an hour after Bonham arrived the 3 long awaited units marched into San Antonio : The Aldama Battalion, the Toluca Battalion and the Zapadore Battalion which was made up of the engineers of all the companies in Gaona's force. The engineers carried axes in addition to the muskets. Axes to chop down doors and gates. They would find plenty of doors in the Alamo. These were the best infantry units the Dictator had. Now he would be able to take that poor excuse of a fort. Now he could get on with the campaign and crush this rebellion. Too long this place had delayed him.

The Dictator now had over 3,000 men. Other historians have claimed 1,500. Evidently their adding machines need oiling. Present on the 3rd of March:

INFANTRY:

Matamoros
Jimenez
San Luis Potosi
Allende
Aldama
Toluca
Zapadores

CAVALRY:

Dolores
Tampico

(plus small mounted units accompanying most battalions. i.e. the Aldama Chasseurs, etc.)

The word went out that Smith would be riding out tonight. Any letters should be given to him. Soon everyone was busy writing relatives. One letter tells us what was on the minds of the defenders:

"*...the Mexicans keep marching with their new blue and red uniforms.*"[22]

And he tells us that Travis is going to call a meeting later today:

"Travis is going to call us together tonight. I hope he changes the defenses." [23]

There has been a tendency to picture the Mexican army in 1836 as an motley, ragged, mob. In Onderdonk's painting CROCKETT'S LAST STAND he shows a Mexican officer wearing a sombrero with a cigar clinched in his teeth. About the only correct thing he shows about the soldiers is their sandles. Even the British in the Peninsula campaigns wore them. But in this winter weather they must have been a misery.

Let there be no doubt. The Mexican army at the Alamo was well uniformed. And the only sombreros there were worn by the women followers who did the cooking and laundry.

One of Travis' letters written on this day gives his state of mind. He is now angry with the local Mexicans for abandoning him:

"The citizens of this municipality are all our enemies, except those who have joined us heretofore. We have three Mexicans now in the fort; those who have not joined with us in this extremity, should be declared public enemies, and their property should aid in paying the expenses of the war." [24]

This is the lawyer in Travis speaking. But what did he tell his men in the meeting we know he held that night ? The men were not blind. They knew Bonham had brought news. But Travis now misled them, asking them to continue the struggle a little longer. And he would have commented on the betrayal of the local Mexicans. That flag with two stars no longer was appropriate. One of those stars did not belong there. Texas was clearly fighting alone. Coahuila had not risen in revolt to aid them. Perhaps now he had a man lower the flag and rip off a star. It would have been a dramatic gesture. It would have been typical of Travis with his flair for the dramatic.

One star was left. One star stood alone on a Mexican flag – the Mexico that had betrayed them and the Constitution of 1824. This lone star of Texas was what they were fighting for now. It was what he was asking them to die for. It was to be Travis' finest hour. He had done what had to be done.

On this day Houston was appointed Commander in Chief.

MARCH 4, Friday

The Dictator Plans The Final Assault

The day began with wind but became a nice 42 degrees.

Mexican artillery opened fire early. The northern battery of 4 had been moved to within 250 yards during the night. Every shot hit the north wall. Two more 9 pounders worked on the west wall but they were a good 400 yards away.

Another Travis letter, written on March 3rd, tells us where the surrounding trenches were located : On the west 400 yards. To the southeast 1,000 yards. To the southwest 300 yards where they went behind La Villita's ruins. To the northeast 800 yards on the irrigation ditch; to the north 800 yards at the old Mill. Remember, these were the infantry trenches.

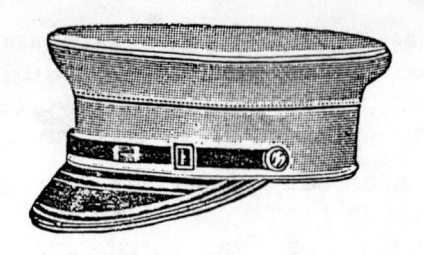

MILITARY CAP. *This style was worn by the New Orleans Grays in the Alamo.*

Travis was giving precise locations because he wanted to help anyone trying to aid him. These details also tell us he still, on March 3rd, hoped there might be help coming from somewhere.

Mortars lobbed shells into the plaza area, blowing out craters and doing no real damage. Sometimes the fuses went out and the Alamo men were able to measure the dud shells. They were being bombarded by 2 sizes of mortars: $5\frac{1}{2}$ inch and 8 inch. We can guess that Jameson and Dickinson took these shells apart to fire the contents back during the final assault.

In the afternoon the Alamo fired 2 cannon and they could have been testing some previously unfired pieces. It was good weather to dig and shifts of defenders shoveled dirt and made sandbags. The inner side of the northern wall was reinforced. A battery near the center of the wall was moved to the corner, covering a blind spot. They were also making an trench (from which came the dirt) on the inner side of that wall.

Map A shows a outside trench was started on the north wall, beginning at the east corner. These outside trenches were dug at night but the inside work could be done anytime.

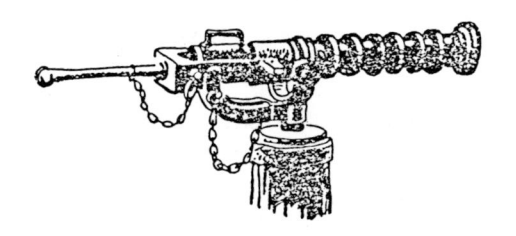

SWIVEL GUN (Spanish). *Three of these were above the south gate in an watchtower structure reinforced with sandbags.*

By attacking at night or in pre-dawn, the Dictator wouldn't have to fight for those ditches. This fact alone should have foretold when the final assault would come. Travis was not able to man the ditches at night because there was no way to prevent a storming in the dark.

The northern batteries were being moved 50 yards closer each night. Evidently the Dictator had decided to make a breach in the north wall. A breach was very important in the taking of fortified positions. Generals and military 'experts' discussed the matter endlessly. Technically, once a breach was made - that is, a section of a defensive wall knocked down - an order for the defenders to surrender was supposed to be made. And if they refused the attackers then owed them no mercy.

Wellington lost over 2,000 men trying to fight past a blocked breach in Spain at Ciudad Rodrigo. He later said if they had then killed all the defenders he wouldn't have had to fight so hard to take Badajoz.[25] What he meant was that had he made an example of Ciudad Rodrigo (killing all the French without mercy) then when he asked the next fort (Badajoz) to surrender after a breach - they would have.

Clearly, the Dictator was trying to make a breach in that north wall with his little 9 pounders. He was moving them steadily closer in order to fire point blank (directly) at the wall. Jameson was in charge of the Alamo defensive engineering and he was using wooden braces to hold loose dirt in place along weak sections of the north wall.

I have waited until now to discuss this concept of breaching walls because it shall figure tonight in the Dictator's decision to storm the Alamo on the 6th.

At this meeting there were representatives from all the Battalions (except the mystery Battalion) plus his staff officers. Castrillon wanted to wait until the two 12 pounders arrived on the 7th in order to use them to destroy the outer walls. Sesma also wanted to wait which is strange because he usually had the same opinion as the Dictator. Perhaps this was just Sesma's way of telling his master he didn't want to lead a storming party when an attack was made. If so, it succeeded. There were no other objections so the Dictator announced he had decided to storm it in the pre-dawn of the 6th.

Here are the plans for storming the Alamo as decided after this March 4, meeting:

A. *WEST WALL* : *Aldama Battalion with 1 company of San Luis Potosi. 10 scaling ladders.*
B. *NORTH WALL* : *Toluca Battalion with 3 companies of San Luis Potosi. 10 scaling ladders.*
C. *EAST WALL* : *Matamoros & Jimenez Battalions. 6 scaling ladders.*
D. *SOUTH WALL* : *Dismounted cavalrymen and one company San Luis Potosi. 2 scaling ladders.*

Notice that the Allende Battalion isn't mentioned. They were entrenched on the east side of the Alamo and being former rebels, the Dictator must have decided their enthusiasm in attacking these Texas rebels would be less than effective. The Dictator wanted to make an example of the Alamo. He wanted to crush them quickly and completely when the time came.

Yet he held back the best companies in the assault Battalions - the grenadiers- because he knew they could not be replaced. This practice of using the best companies to form a reserve was another custom of the Peninsula campaigns. [26]

There was some apprehension among the Mexican officers. One would approach the Dictator after the meeting and leave us with an unforgetable picture:

"Santa Anna was holding in his hand the leg of a chicken which he was eating, and holding it up, he said: 'What are the lives of soldiers more than of so many chickens? I tell you, the Alamo must fall, and my orders must be obeyed at all hazards. If our soldiers are driven back, the next line in the rear must force those before them forward, and compel them to scale the walls, cost what it may." [27]

On this day the new Texas Commander-in-Chief rode west to see what could be done to help the Alamo. His army was rather small. He had exactly four (4) men.

MARCH 5, Saturday

Travis' Last Speech

A clear, warm day. At noon it is 68 degrees.

The northern battery was moved forward another 50 yards last night. Only 200 yards away from the north wall now. They are barely within rifle range and the artillerymen stay low in their trench.

At 2 P.M. secretary Caro makes copies of the attack orders and now Mexican officers scramble about with their junior officers in tow as they study their paths of attack.

The north wall trembles as each 9 pound ball thuds into it, sending a puff of dust flying with each impact. The two corners of this wall are hit repeatedly with these nine pound sledgehammers.

At 5 P.M. several columns of troops leave San Antonio to take up assault positions. At about the same time the cannons stop firing. It is now that Travis calls a meeting of the defenders. It will be his last speech. Mrs. Dickinson says it was on this day that Travis told them there was no hope of reinforcements coming to help them. More than likely he also said if anyone wanted to leave they could. Moses Rose decided to leave. Rose was a veteran of the Napoleonic wars. He knew when to quit. What we must forever lament is that the man spoke little English. Rose would get away and tell his story to a Texas family. This account gives a long Travis speech which is impossible because Rose couldn't understand English well enough. But there are things he must have *inferred* from the *tone* of Travis's speech.

Rose remembered Travis said something about they had been betrayed. Crockett had been saying this for days. He must have been grinning as Travis repeated it. And there are echoes in Roses's account which remind us of lines from SCOTTISH CHIEFS. Lines like:

"...thy fate shall be my fate; we live or we die together; in the field, the cloister, or the tomb..." 28

Striking words. Words that men can die for (if, unlike Rose, they can understand the language). And Travis would surely have pointed out that they had not lost a single man. He might even have quoted a appropriate line from SCOTTISH CHIEF'S again:

"...Heaven arms the Patriot's hand." 29

Don't misunderstand me - or Travis ; religion is not mentioned once in his diary. But when you are asking men to die with you - then it is usually necessary to mention it.

There are a great many things in the Rose account that simply don't hold up. In fact, W.P. Zuber later admitted he had *added* Travis drawing a line with his sword. How much *more* did Zuber change or add to impress readers ? When a man can't speak or write English very well it is easy to put words in his mouth. But the Rose account does have a few things only a witness could have known :

"Every sick man that could walk arose from his bunk and tottered across the line... (Now follows Bowie asking men to move his cot across the line)... *Then every sick man that could not walk made the same request, and had his bunk moved in like manner."* 30

Yes, we have already said that Zuder admitted he made up the drawing of the line but what I am showing here is that Rose tells us there were "*sick*" (those 35-50 wounded men ?) men in relatively large numbers in the Alamo.

Rose remembers he looked at the men, once he had made his decision to leave, and this recollection, whether colored by Zuder or not, remains extremely powerful :

"He looked over the area of the fort ; every sick man's berth was at is (sic) *wonted place ; every effective soldier was at his post, as if awaiting orders; he felt as if dreaming."* 31

Here again he mentions what no other historian has told us - a large number of 'sick' (read that *'wounded'*)men were in the Alamo and evidently they were assigned posts and had weapons.

So not only Mrs. Dickinson and Doctor Sutherland said there are a large number of wounded men there - so does Rose. And he seems to dwell on them. Was this because he felt guilty most of all at abandoning *them* ?

Some historians have Rose leaving on March 3, but Mrs Dickinson remembered he left on the evening *before* the final assault and she ties it in with Travis's last speech. Zuder also had Rose leaving on the 3rd, but how on earth would the man have known what day of the month he left ? And would he have cared ?

Mexican accounts show the shelling ceased about 5 P.M. on the 5th. This would have given Travis an opportunity to call a meeting and give the men a last pep talk. At this late date, with day after day of pounding on that north wall, it would have been obvious to a child that the main attack would probably be aimed at that north wall. And the attack was going to be soon. Mrs. Dickinson mentions 3 'spies' who entered the fort before the final assault and she says they warned Travis that the attack was coming. She also says they died with everyone else on the 6th.

Tonight the Mexican columns are shifting to their assigned attack positions. And who commands the mounted cavalry ? Why, Sesma, of course. He was to prevent anyone from escaping. The prize plum (and safest) had been given to the Dictator's pet General. How all the other officers must have gashed their teeth as that worthy rode by.

NOTES

1. P.101, Castaneda, MEXICAN SIDE OF THE TEXAN REVOLUTION.
2. P.138, DeShields, TALL MEN ...
3. Pp.93-94, Morphis, HISTORY OF TEXAS.
4. P. 212, Jomini, ART OF WAR
5. James, Garry, "The Historic Baker Rifle," Guns & Ammo Mag., Nov. 1983.
6. P.101, Castaneda, MEXICAN SIDE OF THE....
7. P.81, Lord, Walter, A TIME TO STAND.
8. P.524, Potter, R.M., Texas Almanic 1868.
9. Almonte, Juan N., Journal.
10. Ibid.
11. P.77, Brister, Louis E., IN MEXICAN PRISIONS.
12. P.85, Lord, Walter, A TIME TO STAND.
13. P.156, DeShields, TALL MEN WITH LONG RIFLES.
14. Ibid.
15. P.130, Porter, Jane, SCOTTISH CHIEFS.
16. P.69, Lord, Walter, A TIME TO STAND.
17. Almonte, Juan N., Journal.
18. 1860 Texas Almanic.
19. Ibid.
20. P.96, Lord, Walter, A TIME TO STAND.
21. Letter, Isaac Millsaps.
22. Ibid.
23. Ibid.
24. P. 114, Tinkle, Lon, THE ALAMO.
25. P. 388, Holmes, Richard, ACTS OF WAR
26. P.11, Haythornthwaite, Philip, UNIFORMS OF THE PENINSULAR WAR.
27. Pp.173-174, Texas Almanic 1859.
28. P.446, Porter, Jane, SCOTTISH CHIEFS.
29. P.94, Ibid.
30. Zuber account, Texas Almanic 1873.
31. Ibid.

FIRST ATTACK at about 5 A.M. March 6.
Each ───── symbol represents a company
of men – three lines deep.

SECOND ATTACK at about 6 A.M.
Notice the southern column is waiting
behind cover near southwest corner.
Santa Anna waits with the Reserves.

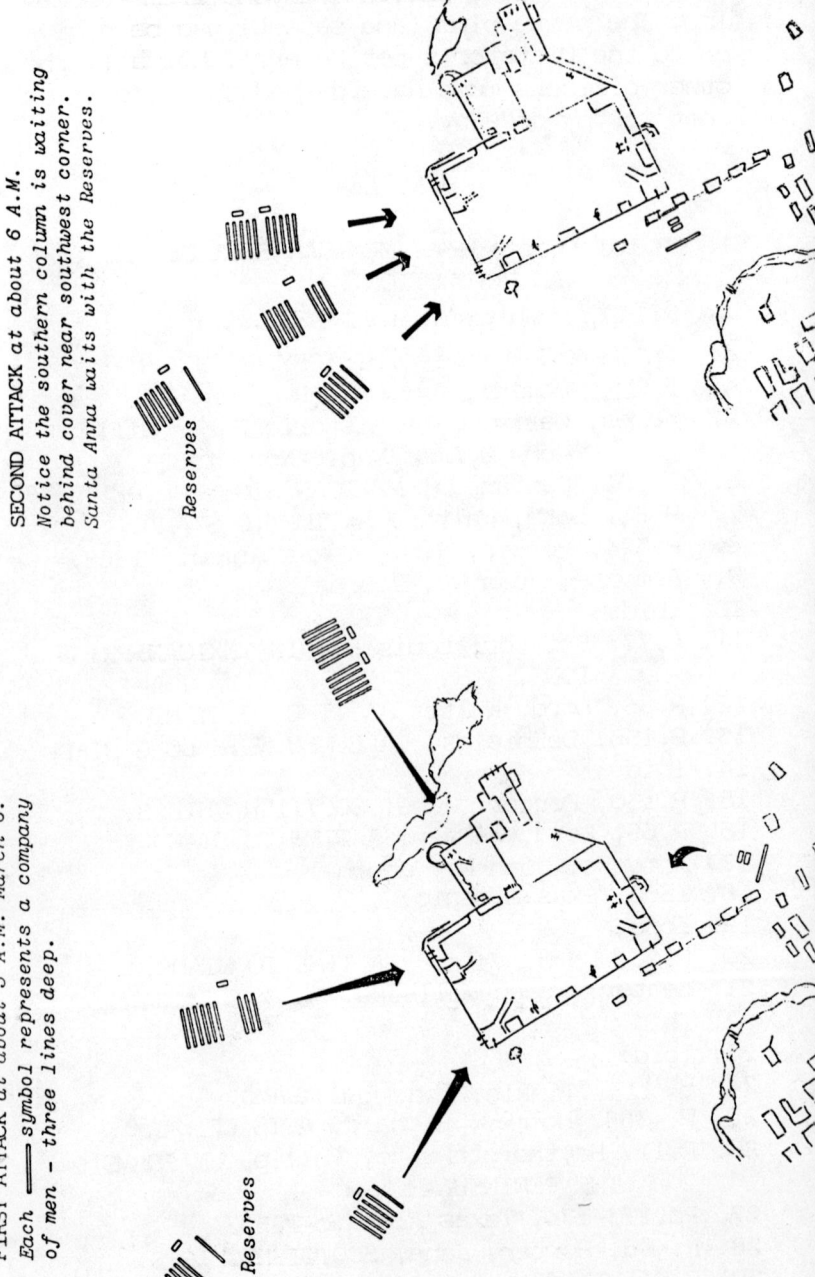

MARCH 6, SUNDAY

THE ALAMO FALLS

5 A.M. and the darkness of night is turning into the grayness of coming dawn. The Dictator waits with the Reserves at the North Battery. His assault plans had been very detailed. With 4 columns attacking all sides of the Alamo he would spread thin their ability to keep all of them from breaking in. The concentration of so much strength on the northern part of the Alamo, however, tells us that he expected the breakthrough to occur there.

Some writers have claimed that a breach had been made yesterday afternoon in the northeast corner of the north wall.[1] I don't think so. Neither did Col. Pena and Capt. Navarro. One commented that evidently the Dictator thought "we could fly over the walls as if with wings."[2] And the other even says that the northern battery was never even used against the north wall.[3] However, in fairness to the Captain, I believe he is referring to the 12 pounders which arrived later but were not used.

But during the night a *wooden* scaffolding had been erected outside the northeast corner. This tells me the cannonfire had begun to crumple the wall there. It was to shore up that *potiential* breach that Jameson had built the wooden support.

Let me clearify this. Wooden bracework on the *outside* of that wall had to have been temporary. Imagine what would have happened if those 9 pounders had opened fire on the wall the morning of the 6th ! Why those metal balls would have smashed the wood into

73

splinters within an hour. Therefore, we must admitt that A. This outer bracing was temporary. B. It therefore had to have been erected last night. C. It was an admission by the defenders that this section of the outer wall was in danger of becoming a breach.

The Dictator made a comment to an aide. He passed a signal to a bugler. As the brass notes split the damp morning air all the columns rose to their feet.

Cries of command could be heard as the soldiers were ordered to straighten their ranks and advance. Each battalion had its own small compliment of cavalry and these small units - numbering only 30-50 men brought up the rear or rode on the flank of their battalion. They were to prevent any desertions and to herd the infantry forward if needed.

What amazes me is the extent to which the Dictator had packed these columns with *extra* manpower. Dismounted cavalrymen were in front of the southern column. The artillery commander was with a northern column and that means his artillerymen, over 100 of them, were with him.

Walter Lord says there were only 1,800 in this last assault.[4] But the only battalion not included in this attack was the Allende unit on the east side. There were at least 3,000- maybe even 3,500 in this assault when we include the Reserves which would eventually be committed.

Trouble at the beginning as some columns were halted and ordered to fire volleys - *before* any shots were fired at them![5] This gave the Alamo men time to get to their posts. To men awakening suddenly in the darkness it must have seemed like a night attack was taking place - the thing they most dreaded.

But Travis had not read SCOTTISH CHIEFS for nothing. There was an item about beacons on castle walls. Much of that wood dragged into the Alamo from La Villita was piled in strategic areas to be lit in event of a night attack. These beacons would have been placed on the roofs of buildings which were against the west, south, and north walls to light the interior of the Alamo. Men who can't see to reload are in trouble and to defend a wall you must first see that wall.

These beacons were ignited as the defenders ran to the walls with extra muskets. Travis would have rushed to the part of the wall any defending commander has to be near: the section the Mexicans had been trying to breach.

Cannons fired as the cries of charging columns gave away their positions. A blast of shrapnel from the northeast battery dropped some 40 men and a piece hit General Dunque in the thigh, allowing his men to come under the command of Castrillon.

The New Orleans Grays were firing muskets as fast as they could bring them up. And when firing at blocks of infantry the 4-5 loaded muskets per man couldn't miss—even in bad light. On the east the Chapel battery of 3 cannons gave Romero's column a triple volley which sent them reeling to the right. And straight into the line of ancient cannon on the roof of the 2 story barracks. Those 6 pieces spit out recovered 9 pound balls. Here is my key scource for there being cannon on that roof aimed eastward:

"(Romero's column) had been sorely punished on its left flank by a battery of three cannon on a barbette that cut a serious breach in its ranks: SINCE IT WAS BEING ATTACKED FRONTALLY AT THE SAME TIME FROM THE HEIGHT OF A POSITION, it was forced to seek a

less bloody entrance, and thus changed its course toward the right angle of the north front." [6]

So the old cannon stopped the attack on the east side. But by shoving this column around to allow it to come against the north wall they may have indirectly led to the fall of the Alamo.

Cos's column was to have hit the west wall but Capt. Navarro's drawing shows they began their advance from a *northwest* position. Naturally they ended up attacking, not their assigned west wall, but the west end of the *north* wall. I also wonder why this column was the only one with crowbars. Did the Dictator entend for his brother-in-law (Cos) to force an entrance through the north gate without informing the other officers of a change in the plans ?

So here at the beginning of the attack we have *THREE* columns ending up against that north wall. Meanwhile, on the south, Crockett and his men gave a nasty greeting to the approaching column. But they would have fired their supply of pre-loaded *muskets*, saving their hard-to-load rifles for last.

This southern column veered left for the cover of some La Villita ruins in front of the *west* corner - anything to get away from the cannon fire and muskets. With his militia experience we can be sure 'Col.' Crockett was directing those muskets in well-aimed volleys. It was important to fire low with muskets and when firing into massed columns shots could pass through several ranks.

Cos's men had not yet reached the Alamo in the gray light when they gave a loud cheer. That cheer gained the attention of every defender on the north wall. Now their cannon and musket fire plowed into the heretofore unscratched column. The cheers changed to screams.

Travis fired down into the masses below the northeast corner. His slave, Joe, fired a pistol. Then Joe says Travis was hit in the head and fell back against a cannon mount. A officer's or cavalryman's pistol must have gotten Travis because other witnesses would comment on how small the wound was.

The Mexicans recoiled from the walls, pulling back in disorder to regroup out of range. During this pause in the attack there must have been a continuous sound of metal ramrods reloading musket after musket along the walls. The 12 pounder in the center of the west wall was moved into a second line of defense, probably opposite the small northern gate to rake any gatecrashers. The westward pointing cannon on the corner battery surely was shifted to aim north because there were no targets to the west on that corner.

There is a good chance the exposed northeast corner (at the corral) was abandoned at this time. Supplying this exposed position with powder must have been a problem.

During that attack the Mexican band at the north battery was playing *El Deguello* ; a hair raising melody which came from the Spanish-Moor wars meaning 'no quarter.' In this period of regrouping the band was silent. *El Deguello* is reproduced in the American Hertiage album HISTORIC MUSIC OF THE AMERICAN WEST and to get the full impact you should play it in the dead of night to let the cold brassy notes send shivers down your back.

Since we are talking about sounds, there is another one we must not overlook. It was a sound which reassured the defenders : The heavy, air-splitting sound of black powder cannon firing. I have heard this sound at Civil War re-enactments and it is impressive. You can experience this air-splitting sound by listening to Telarc Records version of the "1812 Overture." The cannonfire leaps into the 3,000 Hz range and will damage some stereo systems. These deafening sounds must have convinced the defenders that they had a chance against thousands. The firepower these cannon represented was the main reason the mission was considered defensible.

Again the Mexican officers drove their uniformed sheep forward. This time three columns were sent against the north wall. But there was enough light now to see clearly the attackers and all 5 cannon on the north wall fired. The problem was these pieces couldn't be depressed to fire down into soldiers *next* to the wall. But there would have been time for two hurried volleys as the gunners reloaded like men possessed. This rain of shrapnel made the troops lean forward as if in a storm. This is a feature of all attacking armies under fire.[7]

Now the wall errupted in musket fire as the 3 blocks of men came closer, closer, unable to fire while charging. They took the massed firepower of over 100 defenders multiplied three or four since that was how many extra muskets each man had beside him.

Then the Toluca Battalion was up against the wall. Then the 3 companies of San Luis. And all those scaling ladders ? Colonel Pena says he only saw one (1) actually against the north wall. Either the men carrying them had been shot or they had been abandoned earlier during the first attack and were now under the feet of the milling mass at the wall.

The Mexicans were yelling but not as loud as the Alamo men. Y.P. Alsbury would remember Deaf Smith speaking of "the Texan yell" during the burning of Vince's Bridge. [8]This type of yell might have been the strange cry Pena remembered hearing at this wall:

"...desperate, terrible cries..." [9]

Up that wooden bracework climbed Mexicans who used the wood for hand holds. Now we come to something no other historian has mentioned: proof that bayonets were being used by the defenders.

"Our men were thrown back by bayonets." [10]

You can't attach bayonets to *rifles* !! There were fast firing muskets on that north wall and they were firing down at the unprotected masses below. They soon learned not to get up on the wall but would push the muzzles over the edge and fire straight-armed without exposing themselves. For the Mexicans were shooting up at the wall:

"A Texan could not live a moment upon the wall." [11]

For at least 15 minutes, maybe 30, the New Orleans Grays (surely assisted by other groups leaving their quieter posts) held the north wall. The dead eyes of Travis must have seemed to stare at them since he sat against a cannon mount, facing west. Perhaps this is what drove them to yell so defiantly and fight so hard. Travis had kept his word. He had died to hold the Alamo. Now he seemed to be watching, reminding them of the choice they had all made to fight to the end.

To the Dictator the disorganized rabble at the foot of the north wall seemed like a fiasco. 'My God ! Can't we even take this place with 3,000 men ?' he must have thought.

Then he signaled his reserves to attack. Even adding his staff officers to help get his men into the Alamo.

This was the problem. Getting past the outer walls. As Keenan points out in THE FACE OF WAR, men tend to fight hard for *places* because they think of places in terms of ownership.[12] In other words, to the Alamo men, who had been within those walls for 11 days, the mission had become *theirs*.

As the elite troops rushed onto the scene at least one cannon fired at them. Some Dolores cavalrymen were killed. They were riding to the left as the reserves charged. Most of the shrapnel passed overhead. It was as these new forces approached that Cos decided to get his own men out of the way. Cos shifted them to the right. This sent them flowing around the northwest corner and along the west wall.

The beacon fires must have been blazing high now that it was at least 5:45 or maybe 6:15. Cos's men (the Aldama Battalion) were now throwing up 4 ladders against the west wall. The wall was lower once they got past that 11 foot high corner - perhaps 8 feet in places. But the first men up the ladders were *not* infantry. They were Aldama cavalrymen who had dismounted and ran to be in front of the new approach. *THESE ALDAMA CAVALRYMEN BECAME THE FIRST TO ENTER THE ALAMO*. I will soon let you know why I make this statement.

There were too few defenders on this section of wall to stop the sword slashing cavalrymen. Soon the Mexican infantry behind them were dropping into the plaza, getting behind the defenders on the north wall. Others were working on the small north gate to get it open.

There were three horns in the Alamo. One would have been blown now as the signal to pull back into secondary positions. It was also probably the signal for Captain Martin's Gonzales reserves to enter the fight. From their position on top of the 2 story barracks they already saw the Mexicans entering and came running, leaving their rifles up on the sandbagged roof. Martin's men counter-attacked with bayonet tipped muskets.

The north gate opened and the Zapadores and Grendiers of the other 4 Battalions swarmed inside. Too many of them to drive out. The Aldama cavalrymen had even taken the secondary position containing the cannon located behind the north gate.

Col. Pena says some defenders were so surprised they stared at the Mexicans before opening fire.[13] Indeed, the Zapadore Battalion wore red coats. Red coats after seeing so many blue ones must have been eyecatching.

He makes a odd statement but he also tells us something useful :

"...defenders withdrew at once into quarters...not all of them took refuge, for some remained in the open..." [14]

What is clear here is that there *was* an counter attack attempt and that it failed. Too few and too late, Martin's men backed away, firing as they went, as the blue and red flood advanced into the plaza.

Col. Pena says he saw Travis:

"Travis was a tall blond, well built. He would fire and run. He died well." [15]

Remember...Pena says this was *Travis*. We know Travis was already dead but at least we have been given a picture of another defender as the Mexicans advanced down the plaza. It was probably one of Martin's men.

Time now to jump south to Crockett's position. At the sound of the horn he moved his men to the low west wall in front of the chapel (not the west *outer* wall). Dickinson's gunners had already rolled one of their 12 pounders to the gap in this low wall. Another 12 pounder was rolled to the chapel entrance. The fighting at the north wall had given Captain Dickinson time to reposition his artillery. Navarro's map shows a cannon at the gap in this low wall and another in front of the Chapel entrance. Yet the single cannon on Crockett's wooden wall is still there (on his map). The logical conclusion has to be that Dickinson repositioned his cannon to make the best use of them.

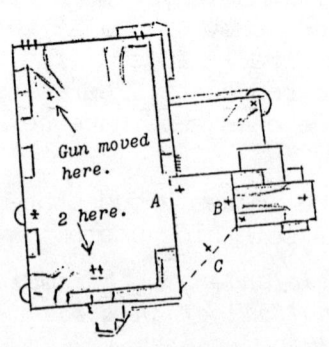

Final deployment

Situation around 6 A.M. as Chapel artillery was shifted in anticipation of north wall breakthrough.

Crockett probably left 2 men with Cannon C to keep an eye on that wall. These 2 men would later try to escape, taking their chances with the cavalry. One may have been the Jackson agent.

But as Crockett aligned his men along the 3-4 foot high wall he saw the big 18 pounder was being turned to fire into the plaza as the Grenadiers came on with bayonets raised high to avoid piercing their own men. It was their last shot. Even as Crockett watched he saw the fur crests of Mexican cavalrymen rise up behind the gunners from atop ladders. Then that long stalled southern column trickled over the southwest corner like a stream.

There was a surviving witness in a room near the south gate. Listen carefully to what she says:

"...I asked my sister to go to the door and request the Mexican soldiers not to fire into the room as it contained women only. Senorita Gertrudis opened the door. She was greeted in offensive language by the soldiers. Her shawl was torn from her shoulders and she rushed back into the room. I stood with my 1 year old son to my chest, supposing he would be motherless soon. The soldiers then demanded of my sister, "Your money and your husband." She replied, "I have neither money nor husband." About this time a sick man ran up to me and tried to protect me. The soldiers bayoneted him at my side. I think his name was Mitchell.

A young Mexican, pursued by the soldiers, grabed my arm and tried to keep me between himself and his attackers. His grip was broken and 4 or 5 bayonets plunged into his body and nearly as many balls went through his lifeless corpse. The soldiers broke open my trunk and took my money and clothes; also the watches of Col. Travis and other officers."[16]

Now pay special attention to the next event she remembers:

"A Mexican officer appeared on the scene. He excitedly inquired, 'How did you come here? What are you doing here anyway? WHERE IS THE ENTRANCE TO THE FORT?' He made me pass out of the room over a cannon standing near

the door. He told me to remain there and he would have me sent to President Santa Anna. Another officer came up and asked, 'What are you doing here ?' I replied, 'An officer ordered us to remain here and he would have us sent to the President.' 'President ! The devil. Don't you see they are about to fire that cannon ? Leave.' " [17]

This seems to be the first time Mrs. Alsbury's account has been published and it is quite revealing. The officers in the account are probably MORALES and MINON. The cannon they have placed near the doorway is one of those captured from the defenders, probably a small piece associated with defense of the south gate. We can guess that it was about to be fired at the 2 story barracks. And it would have been loaded with round shot since the plaza was already filled with Mexicans. Shrapnel would have had no effect against the barracks at that range.

Most amazing of all is that the first officer asks "Where is the entrance to the fort ?" In other words, "Where is the south gate ?" To me this means he wants to open it to admit the rest of the southern column quickly. The ladders against the southwest corner were too slow. He would also be able to tell the Dictator later that they 'took' the south gate.

When Col. Pena's Zapadores reached the southern end of the plaza:

"... Col. Morales ...had taken refuge in the trenches he had overrun trying to inflict damage on the enemy without harming us." [18]

Those trenches were behind (i.e. inside) the south gate. Morales had used the trenches for his own men. Pena thought he did this to avoid being hit by other Mexicans in the plaza. But the real reason was probably gunfire from Crockett's men, the 12 pounder Dickinson had moved to the low wall, and riflefire from the tall barracks.

Cos's men (Aldama Battalion) went after the houses against the west wall. Holes had been made in the rooms to allow defenders not only to fire into the plaza but into the rooms adjoining them. Now defenders were firing into the massed infantry, milling about in the plaza. It was a slaughter pen. Up on the tall barracks roof the Gonzales riflemen were dropping their targets, trying to pick out officers, but usually getting the sword carrying cavalrymen.

Gen. Ampudia, the artillery commander, had his cannoneers to use captured Alamo cannon to fire point-blank at doors. Then storming parties would advance into the smoke filled rooms. He began this process on the north side with the Low Barracks.

Zapadores would have assaulted other doors with their axes but gunfire coming from loopholes must have made this a very costly idea. Semi-circular shields of packed dirt had been built behind those doors, allowing defenders with bayoneted muskets to meet the door crashers with steel and shot.

The rooms in the Long and Tall Barracks were also connected with each other and it is likely there was some withdrawal of defenders from the northernmost rooms towards the Tall Barracks as the fighting progressed.

Bowie was still in a back room to the right of the south gate. Mrs Alsbury says:

"Col. Bowie was very sick of typhoid fever. For that reason he thought it prudent to be removed from the part of the building occupied by me. A couple of soldiers carried him away..." [19]

We know from other witnesses where he was taken. Notice she says *'soldiers'* took him away. Obviously they were in uniforms or she wouldn't have called them that. And only the New Orleans Grays wore uniforms in the Alamo.

So it was now that the dashing cavalrymen of the southern column rushed into the building where Bowie waited in a back room. His door wouldn't have been barred because it had to be done from inside and he was too weak to leave his bed. As the cavalrymen's eyes adjusted to the poor light he must have used the two 41 Cal. pistols (probably percussion) Crockett gave him. Double shotted loads were common for men who knew there would be no reloading.

Was he too weak to use pistols ? If so, then why were they given to him ? We don't know what happened after he fired but we do know he was facing cavalrymen. Mrs Dickinson was later told by local Mexicans that he had been killed by *sabres*. The locals knew since they had been assigned to dispose of bodies. They knew because such information was just the kind they would have taken pains to discover.

Was Bowie able to use his knife ? The Mexican who gave his knife (if it *was* his) to the Moore family said he had been one of the Dictator's soldiers and the knife had fallen from Bowie's belt while being placed on the pyre. And if there was still a knife on Bowie *it means he never drew it.*

But something else is more likely. Suppose the Mexican knife-finder was a local man. I can't see a member of the Dictator's army staying around that part of Texas ! Local Mexicans were also given the task of burying *Mexican casualties* (except for those at the north wall as we shall see) so it makes more sense that what is now the Moore knife was taken from the body of a *Mexican* before burial in a mass grave.

Only the 2 story barracks and Chapel are holding out now. And...Crockett's men on that low wall, clustered about the twelve pounder. They are being rushed by fur helmented cavalrymen of the southern column. Crockett and his party are firing muskets. Some were wounded by now. Time was running out. Most of the men were his neighbors and relatives. He must have blamed himself for this situation they were in. As the infantry advanced he probably ordered his men to pull back to position B - where the other cannon waited.

He did this for them, staying behind to give them a little more time. Maybe there were a few who stayed with him. Perhaps the son-in-laws or men wounded so badly they were reduced to loading muskets for him. We don't know for sure.

What we do know is that Mrs. Dickinson says:

"I recognized Col. Crockett lying dead and mutilated between the church and the 2 story barrack building, and even remember seeing his peculiar cap lying by his side."[20]

She says she saw him and she was there. Later, another person who knew Crockett would give an even more precise location of his body:

"...towards the west, and in the small fort opposite the city, we found the body of Col. Crockett." [21]

A strange combination of words. Before we take it apart let us go over Ruiz's entire statement concerning the bodies of the 3 most famous Alamo figures:

"...(The Dictator) was desirous to have Col. Travis, Bowie, and Crockett shown to him. On the north battery of the fortress lay the lifeless body of Col. Travis on the gun-carriage, shot only in the forehead. Toward the west, and in the small fort opposite the city, we found the body of Col. Crockett. Col. Bowie was found dead in his bed, in one of the rooms of the south side." [22]

Now remember, *HE* knows where he saw Crockett. The problem is in his trying to tell us when we aren't able to read his mind. Crockett was "...towards the west, and in the small fort opposite the city." So he was near that 3-4 foot high wall which was the western side of the 'fort' formed by that wall, the 2 story barracks, wooden wall, and Chapel. " in front of the city" is clarified by looking at Map A which shows this part of the Alamo was "'in front of'" San Antonio.

For some time I thought he meant the southwest wall, perhaps where the 18 pounder had been captured. Or that Ruiz meant the Low Barracks at the south gate which might be called a 'fort' by some. But notice he places Bowie in "the south side." Now if Crockett is in the *same* area he would have *also* used the term "'south"' but he doesn't. Bowie is clearly is *only* leader dying in the southern part of the mission.

You can forget the recent drivel about Crockett surrendering or surviving in an Mexican town. Three people saw his body within the Alamo: Dickinson, Ruiz, and Joe. And all of them knew Crockett when they saw him.

Was this Crockett?

"He...had on a long buckskin coat and a round cap without any bill, made out of fox skin with the long tail hanging down his back. This man apparently had a charmed life. Of

the many soldiers who took deliberate aim at him and fired, not one ever hit him...a lieutenant who had come in over the wall...dealt him a deadly blow with his sword...which felled him to the ground, and in an instant he was pierced by not less than 20 bayonets." [23]

Perhaps the wall the Lieutenant 'came over' was not the outer wall but the low wall near which Ruiz says he found Crockett. And of all the men in the Alamo, only he wore a foxskin cap.

With Crockett's last stand the men at the cannon in the chapel doorway now had a clear field of fire. They swept the area with homemade shrapnel. Keegan points out that irregular shaped projectiles produce very infection prone wounds because by traveling slowly they usually drive fragments of clothing and dirt into the victim.[24] So even the wounds from a homemade load of shrapnel would often result in death at a later date.

Now the Mexicans rushed toward the cannon to prevent it being reloaded. This fight in the chapel doorway finished the last of Crockett's men. By this time the two men standing by the wooden wall were running. Only to be killed by Sesma's cavalry. Even so, one killed a Lieutenant with a shotgun.

But Dickinson's cannoneers were not yet finished. Their 'COME AND GET IT' flag was on the roof above Mrs Dickinson's room. The last 12 pounder had been turned to aim straight at the foot of the inclined ramp. Straight into the men fighting in the doorway. When the Mexicans stormed on into the chapel itself this piece fired into them. Capt. Dickinson would have fallen beside this last gun. There were also men firing from positions on the $22\frac{1}{2}$ ft. face of the chapel wall. One man leaped headfirst with his son, ending their lives quickly.

Now the 11 men in the sandbagged position above the south gate were overwhelmed. Potter quotes a source, saying their 3 small guns killed many cavalrymen.[25] But he mistankenly places them in the chapel. As we have seen, they were at the south gate. After they fell it took the successive deaths of 4 Mexicans to replace the little company flag with a big Mexican tricolor. Some snipers on the 2 story barracks roof were clearly holding out.

Mrs. Dickinson was in a room on the north side of the chapel. Inside was a quantity of low grade gunpowder left by Cos. The plan was to blow up the chapel with as many Mexicans as possible. Mrs. Dickinson spoke of it later and it makes sense if one admitts the goal of the defenders was to kill as many enemies as possible. It also explains why no personal items were left with Mrs. Dickinson.

Lucky for her and the Mexicans the torch man was killed before he could set off an explosion. She was then escorted outside by an officer who called her name. Obviously, someone in San Antonio had asked that she be saved. There was another more important reason : Capt. Dickinson had tied his Masonic apron on her. Most Mexican officers (and the Dictator) were Masons. Masons are supposed to help each other in times of distress.

As Mrs. Dickinson was following the officer across the plaza in front of the chapel she was shot in the right calf. Think about it. The right calf means the bullet was from the 2 story barracks which was on her right. And for a man shooting *down* at a target it is easy to aim too low.

Now why would a Alamo man want to shoot her ? The apron from that angle probably looked like a woman's white undergarment ! In other words, a Texan would have thought she had just been sexually assaulted. Was she now being marched somewhere for others to do the same ? Better to put her out of her misery. But the man aimed too low.

Col. Pena says the "extermination" as he called it, went on for an hour.[26] By this I am sure he is talking about the time spent killing the defenders *after* storming the outer wall. This officer leaves us with an unforgettable picture of the fallen Alamo:

"...that devastated area littered with corpses, with scattered limbs and bullets, with weapons and torn uniforms. Some of these were burning together with the corpses, which produced an unbearable and nauseating odor. The bodies, with their blackened and bloody faces disfigured by a desperate death, their hair and uniforms burning at once, presented a dreadful and truly hellish sight." [27]

At first I couldn't figure out why there would be fires inside the Alamo which was itself made of mud and stone. It was those beacon fires that were still burning. And this matter of uniforms. Pena doesn't make it clear if they are Mexican or those of the Grays. But he does say that many of the defenders' bodies were stripped after the fight by Mexican soldiers. I can understand why they would want to keep uniforms but there would have been no incentive to take the everyday buckskins and rags of the colonial defenders. Therefore it is very probable the Gray's uniforms were salvaged as desirable souvenirs.

The columns of black smoke rose into the clear Sunday sky. Like smoke from the funeral pyres of ancient Greek heroes the smoke billowed upward. Each of the 3 major personalities had gained immortality in death this morning.

For Travis the most fitting tribute now is another reference to SCOTTISH CHIEFS:

"...for they loved in their lives, and in their deaths they shall not be divided." [28]

For Bowie, the dying Gladiator's lingering agonies were over. He and his knives would become world famous. Even other countries would begin manufacturing them. On the walls his unique physical prowess would have added more minutes. But the final issue could not have been in doubt. Defeat was in the cards.

Speaking of cards, Crockett had played his last hand. Jackson's Imps thought they had buried the old fox forever. But his little Almanacs were everywhere and now his death would increase their popularity. For a century he was forgotten until Disney found him in the 50's and Crockett rose Sphinx-like from his ashes.

We say goodbye also to the arch villain - the Dictator. This battle, of which he would say, "it was but a small affair." would cost him the campaign for Texas. Gen. Filisola was second in command and he would later make the statement, *"After the Alamo we never had over 3,000 men in Texas."* [29]

The Alamo battle did not *just*, as so many others have said, delay the main Mexican army. It also decimated the only elite Mexican units : The Aldama and Toluca Battalions along with so many cavalrymen (dismounted).At San Jacinto he had only 50 horsemen supporting his infantry.

As in a grade B movie, events would place the remnants of the Aldama and Toluca Battalions at San Jacinto. And when the avenging Texans swept across the Mexican encampment their cries of 'Me no Alamo' in broken English tells us they *knew* retribution was at hand. The Texans were so furious, one youth, when ordered to stop firing at the running enemy, replied, *"Colonel Wharton, if Jesus Christ were to come down from heaven and order me to quit shooting Santanists, I wouldn't do it, Sir !"* [30]

NOTES

1. Potter, R.M., Texas Almanac 1868.
2. P.55, Pena, WITH SANTA ANNA IN TEXAS.
3. Navarro, notes at end of La Guerra De Tejas
4. P.117, Lord, Walter, A TIME TO STAND.
5. P.47, Pena, WITH SANTA ANNA IN TEXAS.
6. P.48, Ibid.
7. P.244, Keegan, FACE OF BATTLE.
8. Texas Almanac 1860
9. P.49, Pena, WITH SANTA ANNA IN TEXAS.
10. P.48, Ibid.
11. P.149, Myers, John, THE ALAMO.
12. P.164, Keegan, FACE OF BATTLE.
13. P.50, Pena, WITH SANTA ANNA IN TEXAS.
14. Ibid.
15. Ibid.
16. Pp.122-124, John S. Ford Papers.
17. Ibid.
18. P.50, Pena, WITH SANTA ANNA IN TEXAS.
19. Pp.122-124, John S. Ford Papers.
20. P.177, Morphis, HISTORY OF TEXAS.
21. Ruiz, Texas Almanac 1860.
22. Ibid.
23. Sgt. Nunez, Fort Worth GAZETTE, July 12, 1889.
24. P.264, Keegan, FACE OF BATTLE.
25. Potter, Texas Almanac 1868.
26. P.52, Pena, WITH SANTA ANNA IN TEXAS.
27. Ibid.
28. P.503, Porter, Jane, SCOTTISH CHIEFS.
29. P.192, Castaneda, THE MEXICAN SIDE OF...
30. P.140, Winters, "An Account Of The Battle Of San Jacinto," Southwestern Historical Quarterly, July, 1902.

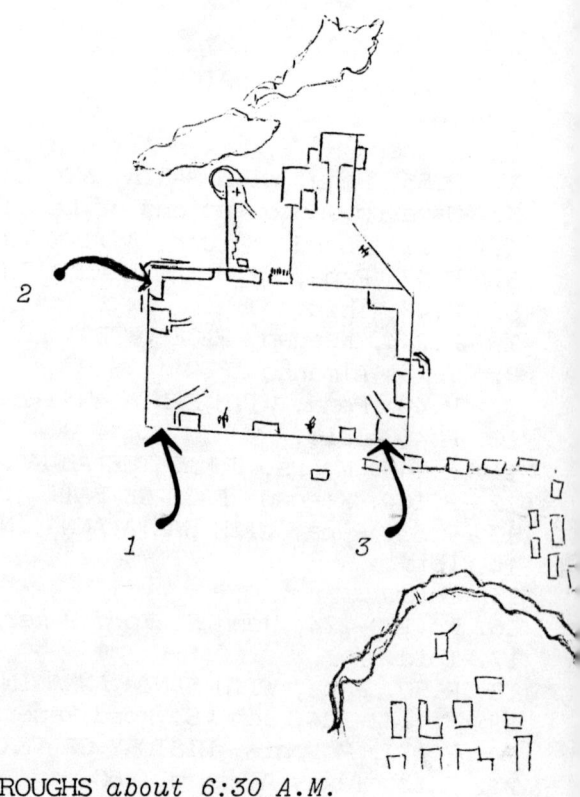

THREE BREAKTHROUGHS about 6:30 A.M.
#1 by Cos's forces which shifted to west corner
#2 by Castrillon's which climbed unopposed over the wooden bracing.
#3 by the southern column when the 18 pounder was shifted to fire north into the plaza.

POSTCRIPT:

The Dictator and some of his staff entered the Alamo through the south gate. Colonel Urissa tells what happened next :

"About 8 O'clock I went into the fort, and saw Santa Anna walking to and fro. As I bowed, he said to me, pointing to the dead, 'These are the chickens. Much blood has been shed; but the battle is over: it was but a small affair.'
I observed Castrion coming out of one of the quarters, leading a venerable-looking old man by the hand; he was tall, his face was red, and stooped forward as he walked. The President stopped abruptly, when Castrion, leaving his prisoner, advanced some 4 or 5 paces towards us, and with his graceful bow, said, 'My General, I have spared the life of this venerable old man, and taken him prisoner.'
Raising his head, Santa Anna replied, 'What right have you to disobey my orders ? I want no prisoners.' and waving his hand to a file of soldiers, he said, 'Soldiers, shoot that man,' and almost instantly he fell, prierced with a volley of balls." [1]

When the Colonel told this story while a prisoner of war he was asked the old man's name. "I believe they called him 'Coket'" was the reply. But this was impossible for several reasons. If Castrillon had *known* this he would have mentioned it when addressing the dictator. 'Red faced' and 'stooped' also can not apply to Crockett. Nor would he have escaped the open battle in front of the chapel or even have *attempted* to do so. He had said repeatedly during the seige that he had no desire to die 'hemmed up.' (i.e. in a building)

The Dictator had the slave, Joe, identify the three Alamo leaders. Then he had Ruiz, the Mayor of San Antonio, identify them. Documents found in Travis's headquarters showed there were 183 men. But Travis never counted the sick and wounded. It was here that Ruiz was heavily enfluenced because obviously some of the staff officers told him what the documents had stated. If Pena knew 183 was on the roll call, then so did the other officers because Pena was *NOT* a favorite of the Dictator.

It was Ruiz who was ordered to use local people to collect the defenders bodies and to burn them. Navarro's Map even shows where this took place: "Where 250 ungrateful colonists were burned." (Note: I do not include it on my detail of his larger map)

But in order to hide the large number of Mexican casualties *the Dictator ordered many to be thrown into the already existing ditches outside the north wall*. Notice the Dictator says in his offical report that "600 colonists were buried in the trenches." Well, there were bodies in the trenches all right, but they weren't colonists !

Ruiz would later say that his people had not only to dispose of the defenders but the Mexicans too. But they didn't bury *all* those Mexicans for several reasons. How can just a few locals dig graves in the cemetary (where he says his group buried most Mexicans after the battle) for well over 1,000 bodies ! And he says there were so many they had to throw some in the river. That adds to my disbelief. The river was the scource of drinking water for the town.

Why are casaulties so important ? The numbers can answer questions.

Items : A. If there were 250 ± defenders killed – that would account for those 35-50 extra wounded men I think were there. Men Travis wouldn't have listed because they were not offically on 'active' duty. Remember, Travis was now an officer in the Texas 'regular army' and a man like Travis took his duties seriously.

B. If only a few hundred Mexicans were killed- then the Alamo siege was a failure for the defenders. But if they took some 1500 with them and wounded another 5-600 then it was a success. Escpecially with the wounded incapaciated and left behind in San Antonio without medical services. Most battles have many more wounded than killed. But the entire Texas Revolution was unique in that the reverse is the case. Even observors at the time noticed it.[2]

C. The Dictator was well aware of the importance of these two sets of figures : his and the defenders. If the rival Mexican politicians learned he had lost 1500+ while killing 250 – then something could be said of the leadership involved in such a battle. Perhaps this is why the casualty report is *not* signed by any officer present during the battle but by General Andrade who *didn't even arrive at San Antonio until March 10*.[3] All he had to do was sign what the Dictator told him !

Col. Pena went to where the defenders had been stacked in layers with wood :

"To count the bodies for myself but the fires were already lit." [4]

But Pena *also* uses the figure of 250 which tells me he talked with some officers who *had* gotten there before the fire. Futhermore, the '250' figure came from someone Pena trusted else he wouldn't have repeated it in his memoirs.

The Dictator had a problem - what to do with the decimated Aldama and Toluca ? Here is where the Allende Battalion comes in. He now disbanded it and used these men to make up their losses. This explains why the Allende unit was not at San Jacinto and was not on Gen. Filisola's list when he tallied what was left after San Jacinto. Not only did Filisola as commander of the Mexican army (after capture of Dictator) *know* what units he had under his command, he lists even tiny units of less than 20 men ! And no Allende unit is there.

My theory would also account for the Dictator's strange comment that he lost at San Jacinto because there were "so many raw recruits in the 500 Cos sent me." These were the reinforcements the Dictator received on the day of the battle - *which were companies of the Aldama and Toluca Battalions.*

March 6 dragged on. That afternoon a review of the troops was held. On this occasion with the entire Mexican army watching, the deserters from the Alamo (night of Feb.25) were brought out to be executed.

General Castrillon protested, pleading that their lives be spared. But the Dictator turned away and his own staff killed them with swords. Pena would later say that one of them was Crockett. Almonte would also echo this but no where in Almonte's daily diary does he mention Crockett or this incident.

Before we look at both accounts of this execution let me ask something that seems so obvious - why would Castrillon try to intervene to save more *Americans* when he had already seen what happened earlier when he tried to save the life of one old defender ? But since these men were (I think) local Mexicans Castrillon thought he might be able to help.

Colonel Pena's account:

"Some 7 men had survived the general carnage and, under protection of Gen. Castrillon they were brought before Santa Anna. Among them was one of great stature, well proportioned, with regular features,... He was the naturalist David Crockett ...Santa Anna answered Castrillon's intervention...with a gesture of indignation and addressing himself to the sappers, the troops clostest to him, ordered his execution. The commanders and officers were outraged at this action and did not support the order, hoping...the men would be spared." [5]

Now Secretary Caro's account:

"Among those killed were 5 who were discovered by General Castrillon hiding after the assault. He took them immediately to the presence of Santa Anna who had come up by this time. He was severely reprimanded for not having killed them on the spot, after which he turned his back upon Castrillon while the soldiers stepped out of ranks to set upon the prisoners until they were all killed." [6]

Notice that Pena's description of "Crockett" doesn't even fit the real Crockett. A drawing of his profile in 1835 shows his nose was rather pronounced. Not a face with 'regular' features. And his surviving vest shows he was not the big man Pena describes. And if Ruiz and Joe had already identified his corpse in the Alamo what was he doing alive many hours after the battle ? Notice that Caro has not mentioned Crockett's name. As secretary , with access to the staff officers and all the camp gossip, here was the one man who we can depend on to tell us if anyone thought Crockett had been executed - and he doesn't mention the name.

Why didn't Ruiz mention this execution to Texans later ? Because they were local Mexicans. They were considered deserters to be buried quickly and forgotten. Caro's story of their being discovered hiding doesn't add up. They had been kept under guard in San Antonio and now the Dictator was going to make examples of them in front of everyone.

Pena commented on the "icy mood" of the gathered troops. If the condemned had been Texans the troops would have cheered their execution. But fellow Mexicans ? No.

After the executions the Dictator gave a speech, praising the bravery of the troops. Col. Pena then tells us something interesting that happened:

"The vivas were seconded icily, and silence would have hardly been broken if I... had not addressed myself to the valiant chasseurs of Aldama, hailing the Republic and them..." [7]

He praised them openly because everyone there knew they were the *first* over the Alamo walls. They were the *real* Mexican heroes. Dismounted Mexican cavalrymen had led in *both* of the breakthroughs of the outer defenses.

The day was ending. Even Captain Navarro, who admired the Dictator, said of this fight, "Another such battle and we will go to the devil." As the real Napoleon once said, "..An extraordinary situation requires extraordinary resolution...How many things apparently impossible have nevertheless been performed by resolute men who had no alternative but death." The real Napoleon would have understood what had happened today. The false Napoleon tried to conceal what happened.

There are still coals glowing in the pyre where the heroes were laid. Who could have known on this March day in 1836, that these coals would always give off light.

NOTES

1. Texas Almanac 1859.
2. Col. Wm. T. Austin, Texas Almanac 1860.
3. P.154, DeShields, TALL MEN WITH LONG RIFLES.
4. P.55, Pena, WITH SANTA ANNA IN TEXAS.
5. P.53, Ibid.
6. P.104, Castaneda, Carlos E., THE MEXICAN SIDE OF THE TEXAN REVOLUTION.
7. Pp.52,53, Pena, WITH SANTA ANNA IN TEXAS.

Appendex A

NEW POINTS MADE BY THIS STUDY:

1. Many defenders were armed with U.S. Model 1816 Muskets. These along with the muskets captured from Cos produced most of small arms firepower.

2. The wounded from the Cos battle made total casualties 250 ± not 183 for the defenders.

3. Mexican losses in final assault were at least 1500 killed. Half this number fell at north wall.

4. The Allende Battalion was disbanded to fill depleted Aldama and Toluca Battalions.

5. Crockett died fighting against the west wall of his 'fort' in front of chapel. He wore foxskin cap.

6. Defenders intended to explode chapel once it was filled with attackers.

7. Alamo had three flags. Main one was Mexican Tricolor with 2 white stars. After March 3, one star was probably removed.

8. Most Alamo defenses had been constructed by Cos in December.

9. Crockett's 'Old Betsy' was probably a plain N.C. border rifle. One of Bowie's fighting

knives is probably the Moore knife.

10. The decision to hold the Alamo was mainly due to the large number of cannon there.

11. Among Crockett's party there was probably an informer paid by Jackson's political party to spy on this potential Whig Candidate for president.

12. The 5-7 men executed after the battle were of 9 local Mexicans who had deserted the Alamo earlier.

13. Beacons of firewood were used in the Alamo.

14. Napoleonic tactics and theories were used by both sides. Except for use of the rifles by defenders - the entire battle could have been from Spanish Peninsular wars.

15. Travis called two meetings. One on March 3, and one on March 5, when Rose left.

16. Importance of the battle is not only that they delayed main army but that they destroyed best units: Aldama & Toluca Battalions along with substantial cavalry elements.

17. Battle began at 5 A.M. and was over at 8.

18. Most Mexican losses were buried in Alamo trenches to prevent their being counted.

19. No breach was made in the outer wall.

20. Both penetrations of outer defenses were by dismounted Mexican cavlrymen.

BIBLIOGRAPHY

Almonte, Juan N., The Private Journal, Southwestern Hist. Quarterly. Vol.XLVIII.

Callott, W.H., SANTA ANNA, Univ. of Oklahoma Press, 1936.

Castaneda, Carlos E., THE MEXICAN SIDE OF THE TEXAN REVOLUTION, P.L. Turner, 1928.

Crockett, David, NARRATIVE OF THE LIFE OF DAVID Crockett. (many reprints available)

Day, James M., THE TEXAS ALMANAC 1857-73, Waco Texas, Texian Press, 1967. (contains copies of all related almanac material pertaining to Alamo)

DeShields, James T., TALL MEN WITH LONG RIFLES, Naylor Co., 1935. (many scources not found elsewhere)

Gluckman, Arcadi, IDENTIFYING OLD U.S. MUSKETS, RIFLES, & CARBINES, Stackpole, 1965.

Hanighen, Frank C., SANTA ANNA, Coward-McCann, Inc., 1934.

Dickinson Mrs.(see 'Testimony of mrs Hanning Touching on the Alamo Massacre (Sept. 23, 1876) at Texas State Library at Austin.)

Harkort, Edward, (see IN MEXICAN PRISONS, Translated and Ed. by Louis E. Brister, Texas A&M Univ. Press, 1986)

Haythornthwaite, Philip F., UNIFORMS OF THE PENINSULAR WAR, Blandford Press, 1978.

Held, Robert, THE AGE OF FIREARMS, Harper & Bros 1957.

Hittle, J.D., JOMINI"S ART OF WAR,Stackpole,1958

Holmes, Richard, ACTS OF WAR : BEHAVIOR OF MEN IN BATTLE, The Free Press, 1985.

Hough, Emerson, THE WAY TO THE WEST, Grosset & Dunlap, 1903.

James, Garry, "The Historic Baker Rifle," GUNS & AMMO MAG., Nov. 1983.

Jomini, THE ART OF WAR, Greenwood Press, 1971.

Keegan, John, THE FACE OF BATTLE, Viking, 1976.

King, Richard C., SUSANNA DICKINSON, Shoal Creek Pub., 1976.

Lord, Walter, A TIME TO STAND, Harper & Bro
       1961, (best general account)
Manucy, Albert, ARTILLERY THROUGH THE AGES,
       Nat. Park Service, 1985.
Maverick, Mary A., MEMOIRS, Alamo Printing
       Co., 1921.
Morphis, J.M., HISTORY OF TEXAS, U.S. Pub.
       Co., 1875.
Morfi, Fray Juan A., HISTORY OF TEXAS 1673-
       1779, Quivira Society, 1935.
Myers, John, THE ALAMO, E.P. Dutton, 1948.
Navarro, Carlos S., LA GUERRA DE TEJAS,
       Editorial Jus, S.A. Mexico, 1960.
Pena, Jose E. WITH SANTA ANNA IN TEXAS, Trans
       lated & Ed. by Carmen Perry, Texas
       A&M Univ. Press, 1975.
Porter, Jane, THE SCOTTISH CHIEFS, Ed. by
       Kate wiggin & Nora Smith, 1956
       (orig. 1809) Charles Scribner's.
Sibley, Marilyn, TRAVELERS IN TEXAS 1760-
       1860, Univ. of Texas, 1967.
Tinkle, Lon, THE ALAMO,(also titled 13 DAYS
       TO GLORY) McGraw-Hill, 1958.
Travis, William B., DIARY,Edited by Robert
       E. Davis, Texian Press, 1966.
Williamson, Jim, "Is This The Knife From The
       Alamo ?" NATIONAL KNIFE MAG.Dec.'83
Winter, Butch, "The Real Bowie Knife ? Many
       Say Yes," NATIONAL KNIFE MAG. Aug.
       1983.

NOTE: The memoirs of Santa Anna, Caro, and
    others are found in Castaneda's   THE
    MEXICAN SIDE OF THE TEXAN REVOLUTION.

APPENDEX A

MEXICAN OFFICERS AND ENLISTED MEN KNOWN TO HAVE BEEN IN THE TEXAS CAMPAIGN.

This listing is offered to encourage hispanic scholars to research these men. Most were officers and being upper class, would have been likely to have letters, journals, and stories which were repeated and passed down by relatives.

The Mexican angle to the Alamo battle offers the most hope of NEW data on the Alamo story.

Aguado, Francisco : An officer. Rank unknown. Killed after refusing to surrender at San Jacinto.

Aguirre, Marcial Peralta : Lt. Col., Secretary Caro says he was among the first to climb the wooden bracing at the northeast wall during attack. Described as "amiable." Killed at San Jacinto.

Aguirre, Miguel : Capt., Tampico Regt. Commanded Santa Anna's personal guards. Commanded the Mexican cavalry force at San Jacinto. Wounded in thigh, escaped in the battle, saying later the defeat had been 'perfect.'

Alavez, (?) : Capt., Staff officer under Gen. Urrea. Described as honest.

Alcerrica, (?) : Colonel. Tres Villas Battalion. Personally supervised massacre of Fannin prisoners. On hearing of defeat at San Jacinto he deserted his post at Matagorda and fled to Mexico.

Almonte, Juan : Colonel. Head of Staff. Very intelligent. Well educated. Voted for the March 6, assault. Later said, "Another such victory will ruin us." Captured at San Jacinto and his journal published in Newspapers.

Alvarado, Miguel : First Sgt. Tres Villas Battalion. Was given emergency command of their Grenadier company when news came of the San Jacinto defeat.

Alvarez, Secundino : Private. Killed on 25. February when ordered by Santa Anna to approach Alamo. San Luis Potosi Battalion.

Amador, Juan Valentin : General. Supposed to have personally led the first breakthrough on the northeast corner. Had 2 days earlier been relieved of duty by Santa Anna. Was Staff Officer. Ordered Alamo cannon to be used against doors of Long Barracks.

Amat, Agustin : Colonel. Staff Officer. Led the Zapadores in Alamo assault. At March 4, meeting he was undecided about attack for 6th.

Ampudia, Pedro : Lt. Col. Commanded artillery during the seige. Said to have been among the first to "gain foothold" on north wall. Told everyone he was a Cuban. Once inside Alamo he used Alamo artillery against entrenched defenders.

Andrade, Juan Jose : General. Once fought in the civil wars against Santa Anna. Reached Alamo on March 10. Some confusion concerning cavalry units he commanded. Since his Tampico unit was already at Alamo he proceeded with 2 smaller units. Horses probably pooled to premit more famous Tampico unit to go on. Signed offical casualty report of 311 Mexican & 600 Texans killed.

Arago, Juan : Maj. General. Frenchman. Arrived at Alamo March 9 in bad health. On Dec. 18 1835, Santa Anna made him Major General of entire army. Some officers believed campaign in Texas would have "been different" if he could have made observations.

Arenal, Ignacio : Lt., Commanded only piece of artillery at San Jacinto.

Avila, Jose Maria : Capt., Commanded the best companies of the Activos of Mexico City Battalion at San Jacinto.

Bachiller, Miguel : Capt., Courier for Santa Anna between army units in Texas.

Barragan, Marcos : Capt. Aide to Santa Anna. Temporary commander of elements of Mexico City Battalion but they were insubordinate. Saved Joe's life (Travis' slave) when found in Alamo.

Batres, Jose : Colonel. Aide to Santa Anna. Remembered Santa Anna tossing Bowie's message (on first day) to him, saying, "The Mexican army cannot come to terms under any conditions with rebellious foreigners..." Killed at San Jacinto while trying to escape.

Becerra, Francisco : Sgt. Claimed 2,000 Mexicans killed and 300 wounded at Alamo.

Bringas, Juan : Colonel. Staff Officer. Fell in creek while crossing bridge to Alamo. Sent to Gen. Gaona to rush forward 3 Battalions. On April 11, he commanded Cazadore unit.

Castrillon, Manuel Fernandez : General. Cuban and veteran of Spanish peninsular wars. Tallest man in Mexican army. Deep voice. Wore blue cloak. Wanted to wait for the 12 pounder artillery to arrive to breach outer walls be- attempting a final assault. Killed at San Jacinto while commanding one of few firing lines to stand firm.

Caspedes, Manuel : Colonel. Commanded Guerrero Battalion at San Jacinto. Escaped and was Acting Major General until replaced by Gen. Woll on April 17.

Cos, Martin Perfecto de : General. Brother-in law of Santa Anna. Felt Alamo wasn't softened up enough to attack. Led column which (on paper) was to hit west wall. Actually hit northwest corner. Led Aldama Battalion.

Delgado, Pedro : Colonel. Staff Officer. Commanded Lt. Arenal and the 6 pounder used at San Jacinto.

Delgado, Trinidad : (?) Chasseur of San Luis Potosi Battalion drowned on March 2, in creek between Alamo and Town.

Dromundo, Ricardo : Colonel. Quartermaster. Brother-in-law of Santa Anna. Never accounted for money susposed to buy food for army.

Dunque, Francisco : Colonel. Led Toluca Battalion. Possibly the *best* battalion. Wounded in thigh but survived because of excellent health at time of injury.

Espinosa, Luis : Rank (?). Fifer of Guerrero Battalion. 12 years old. Hid during San Jacinto battle and escaped the next day.

Esteban, Trinidad Santos : Lt. Guerrero Battalion. Replaced Mora as hospital director because he had *some* knowledge of surgery. Had a "positive attitude." Notice that he was not a physican but was forced to serve as such.

Filisola, Vicent : General. Italian. Reached Alamo March 9 or 10. Second-in-command under Santa Anna. Very stuffy. Protested constantly against women 'cluttering up' the army.

Gaona, Antonio : General. Cuban. Led 2nd Brigade. Most of his unit was rushed forward for final assault on Alamo. Reached Alamo on March 10. Said to be "sullen, irritable, and haughty"

Garay, (?) : Colonel. Urrea's division. Hid some of Fannin's men to prevent their being executed.

Gonzalez, Manuel : Lt. Col. Matamoros Battalion. Wounded at Alamo. Survived.

Gonzales, (?) : Colonel. On March 9, he was ordered to accompany Gen. Sesma to Gonzales with the first troops to leave San Antonio after the Alamo battle.

Gonzalez, Jose Maria : (?) Zapadore Battalion. Trumpeter gave attack signal on March 6.

Heredia, Jose Maria : Sgt. Zapadore Battalion. Wore white hat during the attack as act of daring. Hit by "grapeshot" in the attack and died in great pain 13 days later.

Hernandez, Jacinto : Sgt. Artillery section. During the retreat on June 10, stabbed wife, killing her.

Herrera, Jose Maria : Capt. Toluca Chasseurs. Killed by cannon fire from north wall.

Huerta, Carolino : Capt. Tres Villas Battalion. Personally supervised execution of Fannin. He kept Fannin's watch and money.

Iberry, Jose Castillo : Lt. Col. Aide de camp of Santa Anna. Was sent to Cos to order 500 reinforcements at San Jacinto.

Larumbe, Nestor Guzman : (?) Officer killed at San Jacinto.

Lisola, (?) : Captain. Guadalajara Battalion. Commanded one of the two companies of this Battalion at San Jacinto.

Luelmo, Santiago : (?) Officer killed at San Jacinto.

Machado, (?) : Lt. Col. Quartermaster at San Antonio after Alamo battle.

Mendoza, Jose Maria : Lt. Col. Lost a limb from cannonball during Cos battle in December. Lived because Dr. Grant operated.

Morales, Juan : Colonel. Led column attacking south wall. Assisted by Col. Minon. Re-assigned to Urrea's division after Alamo.

Macotela, Jose Maria : Capt. Toluca Battalion. One of Dunque's Aides. Later wounded in Alamo interior fighting and died not long after.

Martinez, Damasco : Lt. Zapadore Battalion. Killed while changing Gray's company flag for Mexican tricolor.

Martinez, Francisco : Capt. Toluca Battalion. Was appointed Battalion paymaster.

Menchacho, Manuel : Lt. Sent on Feb. 27, to raid Seguin and Flores ranches.

Minon, Jose : Colonel. Commanded San Luis Potosi Battalion. On entering San Antonio on 23, Santa Anna sent him with half the chasseurs to take the church. Later sent by stagecoach to witness execution of Fannin's men.

Montoya (?) : Capt. Under Sesma's command. Later sent to join Urrea where he commanded a Battalion.

Mora, Esteban : Col. Appointed hospital director after Alamo battle. Had position only short time. Said to be "devoid of all human feeling." Secretary Caro says he was among the first to get a foothold on the bracework at the northeast corner. Killed at San Jacinto.

Mora, Ventura : General. Was on line duty at the time of the March 4, meeting. On the 23, he was ordered to reinforce Mission Conception.

Navarro, Jose Juan Sanchez : Capt. Under Cos. Had been active with Morelos Battalion before their defeat by rebels in December at San Antonio. Delegated by Cos to sign the surrender then. Drew extremely detailed map of Alamo as he remembered it on March 6.

Nunez, Felix : Sgt. Said during the Alamo fighting it was so dark in the rooms his men were "killing one another..."

Orisnuela (?) : Colonel. Aldama Battalion. He represented them at March 4, meeting.

Ortega, Juan : Sgt. Dolores Regt. Remembered that on the night of 25, 9 men from the Alamo came over to where entrenchments were being dug and asked to see Santa Anna.

Pavon, Francisco Gonzalez : Gen. (Col. ?) Remained in Gonzales after the Alamo battle to collect cattle and corn from nearby farms.

Pena, Jose de la : Lt. Col. Spent 11 years in Mexican army before Texas campaign. Zapadore Battalion. Extremely anti-Santa Anna. Wore white hat during attack as act of bravado.

Portilla, Manuel de la : (?) Aide to Santa Anna. Brother of Lt. Col. Portilla. Believed killed at San Jacinto.

Portilla, Jose Nicolas de la : Lt. Colonel. Sent by Santa Anna to witness execution of Fannin's men. He also personally decided to additionally execute Ward's 80 men. Urrea left him at Goliad as commander of that post. Later imprisoned in Mexico for some offense.

Sesma, Ramiez y : General. Cuban. On Feb. 22, he was supposed to surprise rebels in San Antonio. Believed a spy who claimed rebels were coming to attack HIM ! Commanded mounted cavalry during Alamo assault. Said to have "Styled himself as Murat."

Rocha, Vallejo : Capt. Guadalajara Battalion. Commanded one of the 2 companies of this unit in San Jacinto battle.

Romero, Felipe : First Adjutant. Commanded Aldama Battalion units at San Jacinto.

Romero, Jose Manuel : Colonel. Matamoros Battalion. Led this unit to attack east wall. Wanted to wait until the 12 pounders arrived. Once over wall he concentrated his attack on northern end of Long Barracks. Also commanded the Matamoros units at San Jacinto.

Ruiz (?) : Capt. Quartermaster of Aldama Battalion. On April 1, proceedings began which accused him of misuse of funds.

Salas, Mariano : Colonel. Romero's second-in command in Alamo attack. Later assigned to Urrea who gave him post at Columbia.

Santos, Guadalupe (Don) : Volunteer. Led 30 hispanic volunteers from Goliad area to assist Urrea in Mission Refugio fight.

Soldana, Rafael : Capt. Tampico Regt. Remembered a man called 'Kwocky' wearing a cap of entirely different pattern.

Somosa (?) : (?) Matamoros Battalion. This officer managed to escape during the San Jacinto battle.

Tola, Luis : Lt. Colonel. Arrived at Alamo on March 11. Chief of Engineering Corps.

Tolsa, Eugenio : General. Cuban. Supposed to command 2ond 'Division' but once his 3 best units were rushed to San Antonio this 'Division was of minor units. He and Gaona arrived at Alamo on March 11, with 1600 men.

Torres, Jose Maria : Lt. Zapadore Battalion. Killed after replacing Gray's company banner with Mexican Tricolor.

Trevino (?) : Colonel. Killed at San Jacinto.

Urizza, Fernando : Capt. Staff Officer. Remembered Castrillon tried to save an old defender's life and thought he might have been Crockett. Wounded at San Jacinto.

Urrea, Jose : General. Best cavalry commander of Texas campaign. Destroyed Dr. Grant's unit and accepted Fannin's surrender after trapping him in the open without water.

Valera (?) : Capt. Tampico Regt. In General Gaona's command. Often served as courier.

Vences (?) : Lt. Toluca Chasseurs. Wounded in Alamo assault by cannonfire from north wall.

Villasana, (?) : 2nd Lt. Aldama Battalion. Wounded in Alamo assault and died later.

Villalba, Manuel : (?) Quartermaster at Thompson's Pass.

Woll. Adrian : General. French. Arrived at Alamo March 10. Assigned Sesma's command and later made Major General.